THE OFFICIAL
PRICE GUIDE

PEANUTS®
Collectibles

MW00465180

Andrea Podley, Charles M. Schulz, and Freddi Margolin at the Peanuts Collector Club Convention, Beagle Fest II, in Santa Rosa, California.

THE OFFICIAL® PRICE GUIDE TO

PEANUTS®
Collectibles

FREDDI MARGOLIN
and
ANDREA PODLEY

FIRST EDITION

HOUSE OF COLLECTIBLES • NEW YORK

Important Notice. All of the information, including valuations, in this book has been compiled from the most reliable sources, and every effort has been made to eliminate errors and questionable data. Nevertheless, the possibility of error, in a work of such immense scope, always exists. The publisher will not be held responsible for losses which may occur in the purchase, sale, or other transaction of items because of information contained herein. Readers who feel they have discovered errors are invited to *write* and inform us, so they may be corrected in subsequent editions. Those seeking further information on the topics covered in this book are advised to refer to the complete line of *Official Price Guides* published by the House of Collectibles.

The illustrations of the *Peanuts*® characters in this book are copyrighted by United Feature Syndicate, Inc. of New York, NY, and cannot be reproduced without permission.

© 1990 by Andrea Podley and Freddi Margolin

All rights reserved under International and Pan-American Copyright Conventions.

Published by: The House of Collectibles
201 East 50th Street
New York, New York 10022

Distributed by Ballantine Books, a division of Random House, Inc., New York, and simultaneously in Canada by Random House of Canada Limited, Toronto.

Manufactured in the United States of America

ISBN: 0-876-37809-2

First Edition: February 1990

10   9   8   7   6   5   4   3   2   1

To my husband,
Phillip,
for his love, support,
friendship, and sense of humor!

—*Andrea Podley*

Dedicated with affection to my daughters, Lisa and Teri,
whose spirit keeps me on my toes.
And to my husband, Bob, for all you are and for
how much you've meant to me "Through The Years."

—*Freddi Margolin*

Surprisingly, in all the volumes that have been written
about the *Peanuts*® characters and their affable creator
Charles M. Schulz, hardly a word has been devoted to the
collectors.

The collector invests so much of himself, his time, his energy, and his money, into the *Peanuts*® scene. It is really to
the welfare of the collectors of *Peanuts*®, present and future, that this book is dedicated.

—*Andrea Podley and Freddi Margolin*

Table
of
Contents

Foreword

One morning while driving to my studio, I noticed a decal of Yosemite Sam on the back window of the truck in front of me. I was suddenly reminded of how much people love cartoon characters. Even though most of us can remember very little that Yosemite Sam ever said and did, he obviously meant something to the driver of the truck.

When I was about nine years old, I wanted a Mickey Mouse watch almost as much as I wanted a Flexible Flier. When I finally saved the $2.50 to buy the watch, the jeweler talked my mother and me out of it, saying that for another dollar, I could get a watch of much better quality. I still don't know why I gave in.

I used to accommodate the other students in our class by drawing the Disney characters on the covers of their loose-leaf binders because such decorated binders were not then available. This was also true of the Buck Rogers characters my friends and I followed avidly and would love to have had authentic flying belts to strap on our backs or rocket pistols to fire. Such items, of course, were not licensed or available. Instead, I used to draw them on heavy pieces of cardboard and then cut them out for us to use. It is easy to criticize the many licensed products now available, but it is also easy to forget how much we all like to have something as a reminder of characters that we follow every day in the newspapers.

Charles M. Schulz

Acknowledgments

If you are going to do a book about *Peanuts*,® it helps to have a good relationship with the people at United Media. Fortunately for us we did. It was a pleasure working with Vice President George Pipal, based on the West Coast, who helped us in a dozen different ways. From beginning to end, he served as a constant source of energy, knowledge, and humor. We are also grateful to Liz Dunn and Jill Decker of the New York office, who were *equally* helpful with their time and expertise whenever we needed them. Other people from United Media who came to our aid were Carolann Lawless, Barbara McLaughlin, and Patty Hennessy.

We also wish to thank the following people and their companies, many of whom believed in this book almost as much as we did, who took time out from their busy work schedules to provide us with the histories, backgrounds, and dates we needed to ensure the accuracy of our material. No request was too small to be declined:

Bill Lichtenstein (President, International Trading Technology, Inc.; formerly with Aviva Toys); Elliot Steinberg (President of Skore, a division of Eskor Industries; formerly President of Aviva Enterprises); Don Fraser (President, Inetics, Inc.; formerly with Aviva Enterprises); Jill Romeo King, manager of the New York store, and Ralph Destino, chairman (Cartier, Inc.); Evelyn Ellison (Creative Associates); Jerry Weiss (Colorforms); Connie Boucher, chairman, and Chiyo Adaci (Determined Productions); Pam Berkon (Eskor Industries); Willa Jones and Roger Emley (Hallmark Cards); Wayne Charness and Alicia Klein (Hasbro); Miriam B. Gittelson (Importaid, Inc.; formerly with Ideal Toys); Linda Thompson (Interstate Brands Corp.); Pauline George (Kenner Products); Cathy Gill (The Thermos Co., formerly King Thermos); Cathy Arranaga, Michelle Peugeot, and Debbie Hanabark (Mattel); Mark Morris and Diane A. Caffrey (Milton Bradley); Lisa Howell (Quantasia); Barbara Townsend and Phoebe Hummel (Schmid); Vincent Marchica (Synergistics); Tiderider, Inc.; Susie Watson and Betty Guerrera (Timex, Inc.); Helyn Rippert (United Features Syndicated, retired); and to Clayton Anderson (Andy Crafts).

Several collectors and friends came to our rescue when we needed their help. They include Tom Bernagozzi, Gene Christian, Kathy Hardy, Phyllis Horowitt, Linda and Lou Ingenito (Douglaston Party Shop), Susan Jensen, Lynne and Jay Kass, George Kerrigan, Christine Koepke, Margaret Kunitsky, Lisa and Teri Margolin, David Nosanchuk, Patty Orgera, Barbara Palumbo, Herman Podley, Rosemary Scioscia (Creative Expressions), Janet Tuccillo, and Barbara and Jack Wolosin.

Thank you, Dorothy Harris, Editor-in-Chief at House of Collectibles, who believed in this book, and Cindy Berman, for all her efforts on this project. Hugs and kisses to our editor Barbara Goldstein, whose patience and guidance over a long period of time will always be appreciated.

The authors wish to thank Charles M. Schulz Creative Associates of Santa Rosa, California, and United Feature Syndicate for their assistance and cooperation in the preparation of this book.

No collectible guide with as many pictures as this one could be attempted without the services of a top-notch photographer. We were fortunate to have two, Peter A. Torres on the West Coast and Tabaranza on the East Coast. Each brought unmatched professionalism and dedication to his work. No amount of praise would be too much for them.

Introduction

It all began in 1950 as a comic strip about kids and a beagle named Snoopy. Through the years the strip became a stepping stone to a world of dolls, clothes, music boxes, toys, games, TV specials (63 in 12 languages), life-size cartoon characters at Knotts Berry Farm, and big colorful balloons of Snoopy and Woodstock at the Macy's Thanksgiving Day parade.

Although *Peanuts*® characters, their antics and their spinoffs, provided sheer delight to millions of kids worldwide, it remained for adults to catch the emotional fervor. In the real world of big kids and adults (very often they are one and the same), *Peanuts*® proved to be very serious fun and many people of all ages became enchanted with the entire *Peanuts*® mystique.

Not only were people entertained by *Peanuts*®, they were stimulated intellectually, philosophically, and theologically. When they could no longer withstand the serendipitous impacts on their senses, they succumbed to the wonder of it all—and became collectors.

With the step up into the world of collecting came the need for more information. Product knowledge was sketchy. Pricing sometimes seemed as if it was based more on fancy than on fact. Dealers, through no fault of their own, were at sea as much as the rest of us. They particularly seemed impressed by copyright dates. If the copyright date was old they reasoned the item itself was older—and therefore worth more.

The copyright date, as we shall see later, has no bearing on the age or value of a *Peanuts*® collectible. But till now, how was one to know?

It became apparent that there was a need for a guide that was not only a good yardstick for pricing, but which offered relevant information about *Peanuts*® as well.

To our old-time fellow collectors, we hope you will find our work to be the aid you've been looking for, oh these many years. To new collectors, we are sure you will catch the *Peanuts*® spirit and come to believe, as we do, that *Peanuts*® characters have so much to offer as collectible items.

One such benefit is a sense of eternal youth. The *Peanuts*® kids and the thinking man's beagle, Snoopy, are now 40 years old. The 40 years have come and gone, yet they continue to make us feel so young.

Part I

Overview

Scope
of Book

There is a limit to everything.

As much as we love collecting *Peanuts®* memorabilia and as much as we have to share with you, time, space available, and the patience of our publisher make it necessary to limit the scope of this guide.

There is a whole world of *Peanuts* collectibles out there. Enthusiasm for Snoopy, Charlie Brown, and the gang is high in Europe and South America. In Japan it probably exceeds even that of the United States. Japanese products, especially crafted things like baby furniture and beautifully designed ceramics, are truly treasures. The Japanese are prolific in producing *Peanuts* items. Pictures of some special foreign items are seen in part of the center section.

It is precisely because of the large quantities of different items manufactured and sold in foreign countries, most of which never reach our shores, that we must limit this guide to collectibles that originally appeared for sale in the United States.

Another decision we made was to use the early 1980s as a cut-off date. Items that appeared later are too new to have greatly appreciated in value, and there are too many of them for the space available. There is one exception to this. Schmid, which created an excellent group of annual music boxes, plates, and bells, gave up its license in 1986. We felt it made sense to complete the series and include them in this guide.

Finally (with the exception of two earlier "sitting" Snoopy plushes), the reader will notice that one of the most popular of all *Peanuts* items ever produced, the Snoopy plush doll, has been ex-

3

cluded from this guide. Our reasoning is quite simple. Many of the plush dolls are still available for sale in the stores today in very much the same form as they first appeared over 20 years ago. It would serve little purpose to include in a guide to collectibles an item that is still in production today.

All About Collecting

WHY PEOPLE COLLECT

The very fact that you picked up this book is an indication of the hold that collecting hobbies have on the populace. Collectors tend to get a little bit fanatical and *Peanuts* collectors are not much different, although we think they have more fun.

Most *Peanuts* collectors we run into seem to be filling personal needs insofar as identification with characters is concerned. There are people out there who admire Snoopy for his ability to adapt to any situation and for his Walter Mitty type of existence. Some identify with the frailness and sensitivity of Woodstock, while some of a more humble stripe see a good deal of themselves in one of America's most lovable losers, Charlie Brown. Others see in themselves Lucy, who can sometimes be such a "fussbudget" and crabby. What's more, some collectors claim to identify with almost all the characters in some way. In other words, they see in themselves a little bit of each character.

Many people rationalize their hobby within economic terms. While they are accumulating their collections they are constantly buying and selling. We call it trading for fun and profit. But whether they trade or simply accumulate items, collectors know that in the past decade their *Peanuts* collection has increased in value and will continue to do so in the future. More than one *Peanuts* collector has sold his collection to help finance college or for some other worthy purpose.

One reason more and more people are collecting *Peanuts*, however, is that it is still very affordable. One need only visit toy shows and flea markets to see the stratospheric levels other collectibles have reached. Except for the rarest of pieces, most *Peanuts* items are still at a price point where they are easily obtainable by beginning collectors.

Paramount over all of the above reasons for collecting is pure enjoyment. *Peanuts* collectors receive genuine satisfaction from their hobby. They consider most of their pieces to be little treasures. They enjoy the quest for new items and they love to browse through the open-air flea markets on pleasant mornings or mix it up with the crowds in an indoor show. They get a thrill on coming across something they need to fill in a set. They enjoy the companionship of other collectors. Some of them, your authors included, plan vacations to cities and even foreign countries with an eye to finding more *Peanuts* collectibles. It definitely makes traveling more fun.

DIFFERENT TYPES OF *PEANUTS* COLLECTIONS

Some collectors, like your authors, have an insatiable appetite and pick up almost anything in sight. Most, however, tend to specialize, picking up an occasional piece outside of their specialty if it really appeals to them.

One of the most popular ways of collecting is by character. For example, some people will pick up everything Snoopy or everything Woodstock they can find, but will completely ignore Charlie Brown and Peppermint Patty.

Materials specialization is another popular collecting method. There are fans who collect only ceramic pieces, while others may be more interested in metal or glass. A more narrow specialty is by pose. An example of this would be "huggies," such as Snoopy hugging Woodstock.

Probably the most common method of collecting is by category. Thus, some homes will be graced with only music boxes, while others might be embellished with a collection of only ceramic plates or planters. Kitchen items are another category for specialization. Baseball motifs are popular these days, and goodness knows Charlie Brown is responsible for enough baseball memorabilia. Another category that we know will keep a collector busy many a winter night is books and printed matter.

Cross-collecting, which is not limited to *Peanuts*, will be touched upon in the section on pricing.

HOW TO START (Tips on Collecting)

Although this section of the guide is meant to be a primer for beginning collectors, more experienced buffs should not overlook it. It will only take a few minutes and chances are there will be an idea or two you will find helpful. If nothing else, consider it a refresher.

Experience is the best teacher. What follows are some tips we have gleaned from a combined total of over 30 years of *Peanuts* collecting. It is our pleasure to pass them on to you.

1. Research. Before you get started seriously, you might want to do some research. Pick up some books by or about Charles Schulz. Read about the history and the evolution of the *Peanuts* characters. To help you in this, you will find a list of recommended reading at the back of this guide. You're already reading the comic strip, but dig into a few more of the cartoon anthologies. Unlike many lists of reading, you'll find ours to be lots of fun. You will find some of the books in bookstores. Others are available in your local library.

2. Join the *Peanuts* Collector Club. Send a self-addressed stamped envelope to the *Peanuts* Collector Club, P.O. Box 94, North Hollywood, CA 91603 for current information on how to join. Members receive a quarterly newsletter which is crammed full of information about collecting and new products available. It may also lead to contact with other members of the club, an excellent way to get started in networking.

3. Don't be hasty. Until you really have a feel for value and what you want from your collection, try not to make expensive purchases. Even if you have to pay a little more for something later on, you will still be way ahead by avoiding expensive mistakes early in the game.

4. Buy current merchandise. Today's purchases may be tomorrow's collectibles. But remember, unless you actually plan to use your acquisition, keep it fresh in the box. Some serious collectors who enjoy playing with their collection will actually buy two of an item, one to use and the other to keep for display.

5. Be prepared. There are a number of things you can do before you even leave your home that will make your visit to a toy show or flea market more productive. Not everyone makes these lengthy preparations every time, but they are important and they are well worth noting.

Bring batteries for testing toys and radios. Most toys take D batteries and radios generally take nine-volt batteries. You will occasionally also need AA or CC batteries. A good idea is to bring self-addressed postcards with you. Pass them out to any dealers you feel would be willing to be on the lookout and let you know if they come across anything interesting. It's always good to have as many people as possible working for you. Some people will be sure to wear a *Peanuts* sweater or shirt to call attention to themselves. And others go so far as to carry a sign of some sort indicating they are looking for *Peanuts* collectibles.

Get there early. There are usually long lines waiting to get into the better shows and flea markets. The experienced collector frequently arrives an hour early to insure being one of the first on line. The desirable pieces are snapped up early in the show and the collector doesn't want to take the chance on missing out on something good.

If you are with your mate or a friend, ask him or her to help you save time by checking out the selections in another part of the show or flea market. We have seen a few collectors carry this to the extreme. They equip their friends with a hand-held walkie-talkie for faster communication if they find something. (Not a bad idea!)

Look not only on the tables, but on the walls and on the floors. A lot of merchandise is actually tossed into a cardboard box and left on the floor under the dealer's display tables. Which reminds us. Don't be afraid to ask if he has something in *Peanuts* other than what is in view. Sometimes he will have an item hidden from view (like in those cardboard boxes). It is also possible that he will have *Peanuts* collectibles at home or in the shop that he didn't bring with him.

Another "don't be afraid" is don't be afraid to bargain. Negotiation is a part of markets and collecting. If you are polite about it, most dealers will not be offended if you ask them if they can do a little better. (And they in turn will politely tell you when enough is enough.)

Once you've found the piece you want to buy, make sure it is in good condition, in working order, and that all the pieces are included.

6. Keep good records of your purchases—the year of acquisition, the price you paid for it, and its condition. More and more people are storing this information in their computers. Keep up with it. This may seem trivial now, but if you really get hooked on collecting then five or ten years from now you'll thank your lucky stars you took our advice.

7. Keep your sense of humor. Some collectors can get so involved they become overly competitive. The next thing they know they have lost the unrestricted sense of enjoyment they were finding in the first place. The world of *Peanuts* is really lots of fun. It definitely can keep you young.

8. Stick to a high code of ethics. If you have an item for sale, describe it accurately and honestly and price it reasonably for your fellow collectors. Answer correspondence. Immediately return items sent to you on consignment if you don't want them. Pay your bills promptly. Follow these four rules and you will soon find a lot of people out there who will be willing to share and trade with you.

WHERE TO FIND *PEANUTS* COLLECTIBLES

Collectible *Peanuts* characters can be found in a variety of places and in a variety of ways. What comes immediately to mind of course are flea markets, thrift shops, toy shows, antique shows, garage sales, and auctions. But there are more ways to add to your collection. Networking and trading information and collectibles with other *Peanuts* collectors is a good idea. The growing *Peanuts* Collectors Club already mentioned is an excellent resource for this. The club was started by Andrea Podley.

Specialized publications such as the *Antique Trader*, P.O. Box 1050, Dubuque, IA 52001 and *Toy Shop*, 700 E. State St., Iola, WI 54990 will very often have classified ads for collectibles and frequent perusal is recommended. You can also insert your own want ad for items you would like to buy or sell.

In connection with buying or selling something sight unseen, it is good to note that most traders, dealers, and collectors are quite open. If an item has a flaw in it, they will tell you. If they say it is "mint in the box" you can usually depend on it. Many will cheerfully take it back without question if you change your mind, so long as you pay the freight and don't make it a regular habit. Almost all will send you a picture of an item and some will even send an item to you for a personal look-see after they get to know you.

One of our favorite methods of collecting is to visit thrift shops and old "mom and pop" gift and toy stores. It can be done anywhere you happen to be, in any neighborhood of any big city or small town that hasn't already been raked over by another *Peanuts* collector, and plenty of untapped areas still remain out there. This is a marvelous way to get additional mileage out of any vacation. It gives you a good excuse to explore places most tourists would otherwise avoid. Using this technique, a collector who finds himself with a couple of days or even a couple of hours on his hands in a strange city will never be bored. And the thrill of making a "find" can actually make it memorable. Don't be afraid to ask the proprietor if he has any old *Peanuts* items lying around.

We have made great "finds" not only by visiting older neighborhoods, but by going to gift shops in older hotels or even sweeping through every terminal building of a large airport. We have found them caked with dust or hidden in stockrooms.

A bonus to this method is reasonable prices because you will only be paying what the item sold for when it was first put on the storekeepers' shelves five or ten years ago. What's nice about this is that everybody is happy. Not only are you delighted with your purchase but the storekeeper is happy because he sold something that is just cluttering up space. For him it is found money. The lucky merchant who reads this book will comb his stockrooms for collectible *Peanuts* items and head straight for a good toy show to make his best deal—either straight sale or on consignment.

Authenticity

Beware of the items that are not genuine. Not only is it illegal to manufacture and sell them, but they usually have absolutely no collectible value whatsoever and are very often of inferior quality.

As difficult as it may be to believe, every licensed *Peanuts* item has the personal imprimatur of Mr. Schulz. He not only gets to see a sample of every category that is marketed, but he insists that only poses he has used in his strips can be "borrowed" by a licensee. And unlike many other cartoonists, he does not have other artists on his staff, so in a way, every *Peanuts* collectible is something of an original.

It is easy to spot a counterfeit or a fake. In some cases, just the look of the character itself is a dead giveaway. As an example, it seems that every purveyor of a stuffed dog calls it a Snoopy. Quite obviously, most of these imitations are so bad you can't even call the vendor dishonest. He can only be accused of wishful thinking.

Somewhere on every item, no matter how small, there will be a line with a copyright date followed by the words "United Feature Syndicate, Inc." Sometimes the name of the licensee (manufacturer or distributor) will appear. And if a product (such as a ceramic plate or mug) involves a drawing of a character, the signature "Schulz" will usually appear. The same holds true for the boxes they come in.

If in doubt, don't buy it. Especially if there is a considerable sum of money involved.

Copyright Information

The biggest confusion among *Peanuts* collectors and dealers arises from the copyright dating, which has nothing to do with the year the product first comes out. *If you are a dealer or a serious collector and you read nothing else in this book, this is the section that is required reading.*

Remember, copyright lines can be misleading. Never assume that the year in the copyright line is the year the product came out. Rather, it's the year that the character "came out" (was first published), at least in that particular incarnation.

Let's take an example: Charlie Brown first appeared in the *Peanuts* comic strip in 1950 and he hasn't changed much since. A product using Charlie Brown will carry a 1950 copyright even if it was first produced in 1989.

One exception: if the Charlie Brown in question is three-dimensional, the year-date for the copyright will be 1966. The Copyright Office says there are so many elements of "new work" in a 3-D version that it must take the year-date of first use.

Thus, Charlie Brown's sister, Sally, is 1960 for 2-D and 1984 for 3-D, Lucy van Pelt 1952 and 1966, her brother, Linus, 1952 and 1966, Schroeder 1951 and 1966, Peppermint Patty 1966 and 1972, Marcie 1971 and 1984, and so forth.

Just when you thought you were beginning to understand the system, here comes Snoopy! The beagle has five different 2-D copyright years. Remember, the Copyright Office requires a new year-date of first use if the appearance of the character is changed so radically that it must be regarded as a "new work."

Snoopy first appeared in the comic strip in 1950. Like most canines, he walked on four feet and sat on his haunches. In 1956, he started dancing, on two feet, with his nose so far in the air that it obscured most of his recognizable features. By 1958, he was walking erect all the time, and although the jut of his jaw or the width of his nose may have changed a bit over the years, the 1958 Snoopy is the one we recognize today. Thus, the 1950 year-date was in use until 1958 (except when Snoopy was doing his mad dance) and the 1958 date is still basic.

So far, so good. Are you ready for two exceptions?

Snoopy first got the Red Baron in the gunsights of his Sopwith Camel in 1965. With his ears tucked under his aviator's cap, goggles over his eyes, and the rest of him hidden by the cowling, he answered none of the phrases used to describe him in his copyright, so 1965 became the year-date for the "Flying Ace" pose.

Fortunately, when NASA chose Snoopy to make his lunar orbit on Apollo 11, his astronaut suit was similar enough to merit the 1965 year-date as well.

In 1971, Joe Cool appeared on the scene. Not only was his appearance altered (and hidden behind his pair of shades), but his personality changed markedly. After much soul-searching, copyright counsel unveiled one more year-date.

Only Snoopy gets such special treatment. Other well-known characters like Woodstock (1965), Pigpen (1954), and Franklin (1968), as well as the lesser-known like Jose Peterson (1967), Molly Volley (1977), and Cry Baby Boobie (1978), get along with a single date of origin.

One last anachronism: let's take the example of a *Peanuts* strip that first was printed in 1989 and the only characters in that particular strip were Charlie Brown (1950) and Snoopy (1958). Your newspaper carried the 1989 year-date in its copyright line, rather than the years in which the characters first appeared. This rule applies only when the strip is reprinted in full, since copyright law regards it as a "new work."

If the drawing of Charlie Brown is "lifted" from the strip and enlarged to grace a poster, the year-date in the copyright line reverts to 1950, the year of his first appearance or publication. Thus, the correct copyright line for the poster would be: © 1950 United Feature Syndicate, Inc., since the Copyright Office requires that the line be made up of the copyright symbol, a "c" in a circle, the year-date of first publication, and the name of the owner of the copyright.

As you see, it has nothing to do with the year the product came out.

Pricing

INTRODUCTION

The free marketplace. It brings together buyers and sellers, each with his own idea of the true worth of an object. Only when each party can refine their ideas and agree on just one price can the transaction be completed. The price the buyer is willing to pay for possession must exactly equal the amount a seller is willing to accept to forego ownership or there is no sale.

Until now there has been a problem in the *Peanuts* collectible field. All too often neither the buyer nor the seller had the guidelines to help them make an informed decision on establishing value. Sales have been based on such criteria as how much the seller paid for it or misinformation about age.

This book is intended to arm you with the knowledge to make a more intelligent appraisal of the worth of a *Peanuts* item which you are about to buy or sell. We will do it in two ways. In the main body we will describe over 800 items and include a guide to the fair market value of each item listed based on reports of sales at flea markets, toy shows, and auctions as gathered by personal observation and from correspondence all over the country.

In the remainder of the introductory pages we will discuss some of the major factors that influence the value of a *Peanuts* collectible— age, rarity, condition, etc.

AGE AS A FACTOR IN ESTABLISHING VALUE

Contrary to popular belief, the age of a Peanuts collectible is not the overriding factor in determining value. We are not dealing with an antique. The oldest collectible in existence, an anthology of Peanuts comic strips, is only 38 years old.

As you read this guide you will come across relatively new pieces that have appreciated greatly in value. You will also find others over 30 years old that are worth little more today than when they were first created.

However, age has more than a passing interest because 1) it does have some small relationship to value, and 2) the age (and history) of an item is certainly of valid interest to the serious collector.

As an aid to identifying the approximate date of an item it is always helpful to know when a character first appeared in the strip. Some of the major characters and the years they first appeared in the strip are: Charlie Brown, Snoopy, Shermy, Patty (original characters 1950); Schroeder (1951); Lucy and Linus (1952); Pigpen (1954); Sally (1960); Frieda (1961); Peppermint Patty (1966); Franklin (1968); Woodstock (1970); Marcie (1971); and Rerun (1972).

Although birds were in the strip for many years, Woodstock did not receive his name until 1970. Therefore, any item which has an identifiable Woodstock had to come out in 1971 or later. His real product popularity began in late 1972 after the release of the movie Snoopy Come Home. (You will notice, when reading the comic strip, that Woodstock often appears with a group of birds that look very similar to him. Rather than saying their names, i.e., Oliver, Conrad, Bill, or Harriet [who are married], we have used the plural "Woodstocks.")

Use of materials can also be a guide to age. As an example, plastic wasn't popular until the 1970s, while wood began to be phased out during the same decade.

Another clue to age will come from the appearances of the characters themselves. It behooves the collector to familiarize himself with the ways in which the characters have changed over the years, but here are a few helpful hints.

The major changes, of course, came with Snoopy himself. He began as a four-legged animal and gradually began to thrust his body upward until by 1958 he was standing erect almost all of the time. Further changes came in the shape of his nose which was still long and narrow in 1958, but by the late 1960s became shorter and fuller.

Most of the characters also changed over the years. Schroeder, Linus, and Sally first appeared in the strip as babies. Charlie Brown and Lucy put on a couple of years in chronological age. And many of the characters got to be a little softer and cuter looking.

It is safe to say that the major changes in appearance of the characters were completed before 1970.

CONDITION

Condition enhances the value of a collection. With Peanuts collect-ibles, as in so many other fields, excellence of condition is a most overriding concern.

Ironically, since many collectors start out as users—to whom con-dition is not always a priority—they must readjust their habits. When they become collectors, they soon learn to prefer the item as un-spoiled as possible and drastically reduce the wear and tear they put on their collectible possessions. Ideally, they should be in a package, be it a box, blister pack or whatever, that has never been opened and which itself is in excellent condition. This is known as "mint in the box" (MIB). To the collector it's a little piece of heaven.

There is one important exception to the MIB rule. It deals with the graphics. What makes the packaging important is that it has printed matter describing the contents or that it contains depictions of the Peanuts characters themselves. Boxes used only for shipping pur-poses, such as those containing clear plastic and/or no graphics, are of little importance to the collector—and are not a consideration in determining value.

If mint condition indicates superior quality, then "good" condi-tion will be just one rung below. If a box is called for, the box will show minor tears and wear spots. If a box isn't called for, the item will have a few minor blemishes or otherwise show some limited sign of wear and tear. In either case, always check to see that all the parts are included.

What happens when a box is called for and is missing, but the item itself is in mint condition? Exactly that. The item is known as "mint," but not "mint in the box." But value is another story. If the item is not readily available then its value will lie somewhere be-tween "good" and "mint in the box." However, if it is easily avail-able the excellence of condition does not help it. You can afford to avoid it. A good example of this is the Coptor Pull by Romper Room. Its mint-in-the-box value is $20 while its mint-out-of-the-box value sinks all the way down to $4.

"Poor" condition indicates major wear and tear, many blemishes or fading. Parts may be missing. In the case of a mechanical object or radio, it will not be in good working order. Naturally, the poorer the condition, the less value an object will have, even a rare one.

RARITY

When demand exceeds supply, prices will tend to go up, and when supply exceeds demand, prices will tend to fall.

Having summarized what most people will consider to be obvious, we would like to discuss some of the factors that influence supply (rarity or availability) and demand within the framework of the *Peanuts* scene.

Rarity and availability are really two sides of the same coin. They both describe the degree of difficulty or easiness in finding an item. It is the reasons for rarity or availability that most interest many collectors.

Availability can usually be tied to production decisions, which in turn can be traced to the manufacturer's perception of the public's demand. Alas, the public's taste is not always the same as the collector's. Collectors want everything. The public plays favorites. The public became so enamored with Snoopy, Charlie Brown, Lucy, and Woodstock that manufacturers produced an abundance of these characters to the virtual exclusion of some of the others. And it is the "other" characters that the collector is looking for, precisely because there are not that many available.

Take, for instance, the baseball banks by Determined. The complete set consists of Snoopy, Lucy, Charlie Brown, Linus, Peppermint Patty, and Schroeder. But Snoopy, Lucy, Charlie Brown, and Linus, being more popular with the public, were reordered by the stores more frequently. Peppermint Patty and Schroeder, on the other hand, were slower to move, so fewer were made. But it's Peppermint Patty and Schroeder that the collectors now need to fill in their sets. With fewer to go around, the market dictates a higher price for these two than for the other four.

Of course, sometimes the manufacturers arbitrarily limit production. (Many of the music boxes, plates, and bells came out in "limited editions.") Or production of some items was limited to only one season or one year. Production problems, distribution problems, damage in shipment, going out of business or just going on to other things are a few of the many reasons that limited numbers of an item were available to the public. In other words, they became scarce or "rare."

There are other meanings to the word "rarity." Many characters are rare in appearance in either the comic strip, memorabilia or both. A good example is the character Violet, whose popularity in the comic strip began to fade at the same time that *Peanuts* products began to become popular with the public, in the early 1960s. Saalfield devoted an entire coloring book to Violet—once—and that was the end of her solo appearances (although she appeared frequently in group scenes for many years thereafter). The upshot is that a 29¢ coloring book is now worth up to $45 in mint condition.

CROSS-COLLECTING

There exists a type of collecting we call cross-collecting. Cross-collectors are interested in broad categories that cut across many other types of collections. For example, a collector of banks will have in his collection metal banks, glass banks, ceramic banks, European banks, antique banks, wood banks, etc. You get the picture—his only interest in *Peanuts* will be in the *Peanuts* banks. This goes for collectors of music boxes, paperweights, lunch boxes, ad infinitum.

Why do we mention this in a section dealing with pricing? Only to make you aware that many *Peanuts* items will be found in unexpected places—and usually at higher prices. The reason for this is that cross-collectors may be more anxious to fill in a set and therefore be willing to pay more for the item than a *Peanuts* collector will. As an example of this, Snoopy on the pumpkin cookie cutter has been known to fetch a higher price among gatherings of cookie cutter collectors than it would normally command among *Peanuts* collectors. Perhaps, as dealers and collectors get more sophisticated and knowledgeable, this disparity will disappear.

What the Price Ranges Indicate

We are limiting our price evaluations to objects that are in either good or excellent (mint) condition. For objects that are in poor condition, we leave it to you to determine if you really want to own them and how much you are willing to pay for them. We recommend that unless the item is really hard to find, such as the Talking Bus by Chein, or you need a piece to temporarily fill in a set until you can find a better one, stay away from it.

After the description of each item we include a price range from low to high. The higher number represents the highest value in mint condition—or mint in the box if the situation warrants it.

The lower number represents value for an item in good condition rather than mint. It also allows for regional differences (prices on the coast generally run a bit higher than inland) and negotiating skills.

As an aid, we have adopted the asterisk system. If a price has an asterisk (*) next to it, then the item should come with its original box in excellent condition (mint in the box) to merit top price. If there is no asterisk next to the price, it indicates the item did not come in its own box or the box adds little or no value to it as a collectible.

One final word on pricing. This book is a "guide" to pricing. By definition, a guide can only lead. It cannot compel. If you find an item that is not priced strictly within the parameters set by this book, you still have three alternatives. One is to pass it up. Another is to negotiate. Third choice, of course, is to complete the transaction if you find the price not to be completely out of line. If you really want the piece, if you believe it will give you pleasure and enhance your collection, and the price is not unreasonable, then by all means—go for it!

Part II

Collectibles

Advertising and Premiums

Advertisers like to associate with a winner.

From the Ford Falcon magazine ads in the early 1960s through the currently popular "Get Met, It Pays" commercials of Metropolitan Life Insurance Co., *Peanuts* characters have been in demand by corporate America to promote its products.

One popular technique of promoting goods and services is to offer "premiums." A premium is something extra offered by the company to induce you to buy its products.

One of the first major companies to use *Peanuts* characters this way was Interstate Brands. Interstate, a major nationwide baker, included *Peanuts* not only in its advertisements, but also in its premium promotions. Through its three bread divisions (Butternut, Mrs. Karl's, and Weber's) and its cake division (Dolly Madison), Interstate offered *Peanuts* premiums either directly with the purchase or through the mail.

Since Interstate divisions were associated with the *Peanuts* gang for approximately 15 years beginning in the early 1970s, there are more Interstate advertising premiums in circulation than from any other company.

In many cases premiums do not show the company which distributed them. For this reason you will sometimes have a difficult time in establishing origin. Our guide to the rescue!

Collectors who are looking for magazine advertisements will sometimes get a double benefit (although they will have to pay for it). As an example, a collector looking for Ford Falcon advertisements will find them in such magazines as the November 5, 1960, *Saturday Evening Post* with Richard Nixon on the cover and the January 13, 1962, edition of the same magazine which has a coveted Norman Rockwell cover.

In each case the market value of the magazine comes more from the demand for the cover itself than from the *Peanuts* collectibility. But it's still a plus for the collector.

COCA COLA

Advertisement. Ad from Coca Cola to offer Sopwith Camel/Albatros, 1973.   *$10–$15*

FORD FALCON

Booklet. "Charlie Brown and His Pals Have. . . . Some Fascinating Facts About Your Falcon." *Peanuts* characters are pictured throughout this book, 1961.   *$30–$40*

Booklet. "A Scrapbook About Your Falcon Prepared by Charlie Brown and His Friends." *Peanuts* characters are pictured throughout this book, 1963. $30–$40

Matchbook. Advertises 1961 Ford Falcon. $5–$7

Saturday Evening Post, November 5, 1960, pg. 93. Cover: Richard Nixon. 1961 Ford Falcon advertisement using the *Peanuts* characters. $10–$12

Saturday Evening Post, January 13, 1962, pg. 7. Cover: Norman Rockwell. 1962 Ford Falcon advertisement using the *Peanuts* characters. $8–$10

INTERSTATE BRANDS (Weber's Bread, Dolly Madison Cakes, Mrs. Karl's, Butternut)

Baseball cards. Six in a set. Dolly Madison, 1983.

Snoopy.	$2.50–$3
Peppermint Patty.	$2.50–$3
Linus.	$2.50–$3
Lucy.	$2.50–$3
Schroeder.	$2.50–$3
Charlie Brown.	$2.50–$3

Bookmark, ruler, and cartoon guide, Snoopy. Plastic. Dolly Madison, 1972. $25–$30

Clip-ons. Each came in red, white, blue or yellow. Plastic, five in a set. Butternut, early 1970s.

Linus, "Cheer Up."	$3–$4
Charlie Brown, "Good Grief."	$3–$4
Lucy, "Kiss Me."	$3–$4
Frieda, "I'm in Love."	$4–$5
Snoopy, "The Prince."	$3–$4

Coin engraved "E Pluribus Snoopy." A prize from Interstate Brands. Bronze, early 1980s. $45–$55

Fabric iron-ons. Six in a set. Interstate Brands, 1972 election.

Snoopy, "Back the Beagle."	$2.50–$3
Snoopy, "Snoopy for President."	$2.50–$3
Snoopy, "Snoopy in '72."	$2.50–$3
Snoopy, "Put Snoopy in the White House."	$2.50–$3
Snoopy, "Vote the Beagle Ticket in '72."	$2.50–$3
Snoopy, "The Beagle for the Job."	$2.50–$3

Garden kit. Features Snoopy and Woodstock. Three clear seed packets stapled to a heavy paper mailing piece. Dolly Madison, 1973.

$12-$15

Hat. Bakery worker's type with Snoopy, Linus, Lucy, Patty, Sally, and Charlie Brown. Weber's Bread, early 1970s. $20-$25

Inflatable beachball. Features Snoopy as a lifeguard. Has the Dolly Madison logo. Dolly Madison, mid 1970s. $10-$15

Inflatables. Mrs. Karl's Bread, 1972.

14″ Snoopy.	$15-$20
15″ Charlie Brown.	$22-$28

Patches. Iron-on, cloth. Mrs. Karl's Bread, 1973.

Schroeder, "Beethoven Lives."	$2-$3
Snoopy as Flying Ace on his house.	$2-$3
Peppermint Patty, "I Love You."	$2-$3
Lucy at her psychiatrist booth.	$2-$3
Linus, "Here Comes the Great Pumpkin."	$2-$3
Pigpen, "Keep America Clean."	$2-$3
Lucy, "I've Got a Big What?"	$2-$3
Woodstock sleeping.	$2-$3
Woodstock on a football.	$2-$3

Patches. Oval-shaped, cotton. Original advertisement shown. Set of five. Interstate Brands, early 1970s. (Pictured clockwise.)

Charlie Brown, "Good Grief."	$3–$5
Linus, "Cheer Up."	$3–$5
Lucy, "Kiss Me."	$3–$5
Snoopy, "The Prince."	$4–$8
Frieda, "I'm in Love."	$5–$8

Stickers. Snoopy with WWI airplanes. Snoopy gives a brief commentary on each plane. Set of eight, Mrs. Karl's Bread, 1975. (First four pictured.)

Morane-Saulnier.	$3–$4
Fokker DR - 1.	$4–$5
Spad - XIII.	$3–$4
Sopwith Camel.	$4–$5

Bristol F2-B. $3–$4

Fokker D VII. $3–$4

Albatros b. Va. $4–$5

Sticker album, for mounting above-described airplane stickers. Cover caption: "WWI Airplane Album." Shows Snoopy as the Flying Ace. Mrs. Karl's Bread, 1975. $5–$7

Store display. Shows Frieda, Linus, Snoopy, Charlie Brown, and Lucy. Dolly Madison is written under base and is not visible, metal. Dolly Madison, early 1970s. $50–$60

Tatoo transfers, newspaper advertisement. Six sets, each containing seven transfers. Mrs. Karl's Bread, 1973.   *Each set $2–$3*

Vegetable seeds. Mrs. Karl's Bread, 1975.

   Snoopy, "Red Red Tomatoes." $3–$4

   Frieda, "Frieda's Ravishing Radishes." $3–$4

   Woodstock, "Woodstock's Farm Fresh Onions." $3–$4

   Charlie Brown, "Charlie Brown's Carrots." $3–$4

   Lucy, "Lucy's Loudmouth Lettuce." $3–$4

   Snoopy, "Snoopy's Super Spinach." $3–$4

RIVAL DOG FOOD

Patch. Fabric, Snoopy at bat. Caption: "Strike Three!" Shown with wrapper promotion, 1974. $10–$15

MIB (Mint In Box): Item in unopened box, box in excellent condition.

Mint Condition: Superior quality, box missing.

Good Condition: All parts are included. Item and/or box shows limited wear and tear.

Poor Condition: Major wear and tear. Parts may be missing.

Avon

From 1968–1975, Avon's army of door-to-door salespeople made washing and bathing more appealing to millions of American kids with its line of personal hygiene products such as soaps, bubble bath, and shampoos featuring the *Peanuts* characters. Most of these products are still easily available to collectors, much of them in mint condition. For this reason we recommend that you bypass the plentiful supply of used out-of-the-box Avons.

Charlie Brown, non-tear shampoo. Charlie Brown figural is wearing a baseball cap and glove, 1969. $15–$25*

Charlie Brown Bath Mitt and Soap. Comes with a sponge mitt in the shape of Charlie Brown, 1969 (see photo on p. 33, top right). $20–$30*

Charlie Brown Brush and Comb. The hairbrush is in the shape of Charlie Brown wearing a cowboy hat, 1971. $12–$18*

Charlie Brown, bubble bath mug. The mug is made of milk glass showing a picture of Charlie Brown on the front. Blue metal cover with white plastic knob, 1969 (see photo above, left). $12–$14*

Great Catch, Charlie Brown, soap holder and soap. Charlie Brown with a removable baseball glove holds the soap. This item is made to hang on the wall, 1974. $12–$17*

Linus, one gel bubble bath, one helpful holder. Rubber partial figure of Linus suctions to the wall and holds a green tube of bath gel, 1968. $25–$30*

Linus, non-tear shampoo. Linus figural is wearing a sailor hat, 1970. $15–$25*

Lucy, shampoo mug. Depicted on the white milk glass mug is Lucy holding a balloon. Yellow metal cover with white plastic knob, 1969 (see photo on previous page, top right). $10–$12*

Lucy Bubble Bath. Lucy figural is wearing a red dress and beanie, 1969. $15–$25*

Peanuts Gang. Yellow Charlie Brown, white Snoopy, and pink Lucy are the three figural soaps included at 1.75 oz. each, 1970. $25–$35*

Schroeder Bubble Bath (must include Beethoven sheet music and paper "bust" of Beethoven, which is inserted on top of the piano). The box is in the shape of Schroeder's piano. He is in a sitting position so when he's removed from the box he fits in front of the piano, 1970 (see photo above, left). $20–$30*

Snoopy, 1 soap, 3 oz., 1 soap dish. Rubber. Snoopy lies on his back and the depressed portion of his tummy holds the soap, 1968.

$10–$15*

Snoopy, liquid soap mug. The container is milk glass and has Snoopy's picture on the front. Comes with red top or blue top. Both tops are metal with white plastic knobs, 1969 (see photo on p. 32, top center).

Red top. $10–$12*
Blue top. $16–$18*

Snoopy Brush and Comb. The brush is in the shape of Snoopy. The comb is white, 1970. $10–$16*

Snoopy Bubble Tub. This is a plastic tub with Snoopy submerged in blue bubbles. Snoopy has a rubber head, 1971 (see photo on previous page, bottom center). $15–$20*

Snoopy Come Home, soap dish and soap. This consists of a plastic raft which holds the soap and a sail with a picture of Snoopy and Woodstock on it, 1973. $12–$17*

Snoopy's Pal, soap dish and soap. The red dish is Snoopy's supper dish and the two white soaps are in the shape of dog bones. A little Woodstock sits on the supper dish, 1973. $15–$25*

Snoopy's Ski Team, bubble bath. Snoopy is on red skis and Woodstock is with him, 1974. $25–$35*

Snoopy & Dog House [sic], non-tear shampoo. Snoopy stands in front of his red house. Turn him and the plastic cap comes off, 1969.
$10–$15*

Snoopy The Flying Ace, bubble bath. Snoopy figural is wearing a blue plastic Flying Ace helmet and green goggles, 1969.
$10–$15*

Snoopy Snow Flyer, bubble bath. Snoopy is on a red sled wearing a white winter sweater. His head is made of rubber, 1972 (see photo on p. 33, bottom right). $15–$20*

Snoopy Surprise Package. Snoopy is made of milk glass, has vinyl ears and a blue plastic baseball cap. Comes in three scents: Excalibur, Wild Country After Shave or Sports Rally Lotion, 1969.
$5–$8*

Woodstock Brush and Comb. The yellow brush is in the shape of Woodstock. The comb is green, 1975. $10–$16*

An asterisk (*) next to a price indicates that the item comes with its original box in excellent condition. If no asterisk is shown, there is no box or the box adds little significant value. Shipping boxes (no graphics) are of no value.

A copyright date indicates the year the character first appeared in a particular incarnation, *not* the year the product first came out.

Banks

Peanuts banks are attractive, colorful, and functional, all of which contributed to a great demand when they were originally manufactured in the early 1970s. The manufacturers met the demand and then some, and because of this great availability many of the banks remain at or near their original selling price.

A case in point is the papier-mâché bank featuring Snoopy on his house in the famous "Dogs are meant to lie in the sun" pose. This bank, first introduced by Determined in 1969, is one of the most successful banks anywhere and has since become a classic. Yet, because the numbers are so plentiful, its value is limited. The pose, incidentally, was also the basis for music boxes, planters, and other items which we talk about in this book.

Other manufacturers of banks included Ideal, Leonard Silver, Anchor Hocking, and Danara (not represented). Banks also appeared as promotions for the Bank of America and Rival Pet Food.

What may be of more interest to you are banks that are part of a series, e.g., fruit banks, sports banks, etc. These usually featured Snoopy who was accompanied occasionally by Woodstock. The top of the line for series banks is referred to as the "baseball series" in which six different characters—Snoopy, Linus, Charlie Brown, Peppermint Patty, Lucy, and Shroeder—are all decked out in baseball gear. Even among these six there is a hierarchy of value, depending on availability. Although Snoopy and Charlie Brown are the most popular with the buying public, their easy availability does little to enhance their value. It is the remaining four in the series that claim the higher prices.

The only other banks which might top these in interest to you are the musical ones from Schmid (see chapter entitled "Music Boxes") and the ceramic Santa by Determined.

CERAMIC

Baby blocks. Determined, Assortment #1505, mid 1970s.

Snoopy with flower in his hand and Snoopy and Woodstock lying on top of doghouse are the two designs appearing in alternating gingham panels. The top portion, where the coin is inserted, shows Snoopy lying on a cloud. $20–$25

Snoopy with various objects, each representing a letter of the alphabet from A to E. $20–$25

Egg. Snoopy is lying on top of white egg which is decorated with little colored flowers. Determined, #1551, late 1970s. $20–$25

Egg-shaped. Determined, #1560, 2″ x 3″, 1976.

Snoopy is lying on top of his doghouse. Woodstock is sleeping in his nest which is on Snoopy's tummy. Caption: "This Has Been a Good Day." $12–$17

Snoopy is being brought flowers by Woodstock. Caption: "How Nice." $12–$17

Snoopy hugging Woodstock. Caption: "Surprise a Friend With a Hug." $12–$17

Snoopy dancing. Caption: "I Feel Free." $12–$17

Figurals. Handpainted in Italy. Determined, 1969. (Lucy figurals pictured.)

Charlie Brown, 8½". $40–$65
Charlie Brown, 6". $30–$50
Linus, 8½". $40–$65
Linus, 6". $30–$50

Lucy, 8½". $55–$70
Lucy, 6". $30–$50

Figurals, handpainted in Italy, comes with different colored collars. Determined, 1969.

Snoopy, 8½". $35–$50
Snoopy, 6". $25–$40

Happy Snoopy Banks. Sitting Snoopy. Determined, mid 1970s.

Snoopy, #1557, 11". $70–$85
Snoopy, #1558, 16". $135–$150
Snoopy, #1556, 6". $10–$15

Hat series. Each features a sitting Snoopy. Determined, 1979.

Snoopy wearing blue tennis visor, #8545. $15–$20

Snoopy wearing black tuxedo and top hat, #8549. $15–$20

Snoopy wearing gold football helmet with blue stripe, #8544.
$13–$18

Snoopy wearing gray hard hat, #8547. $13–$18

Snoopy wearing yellow rain slicker and hat, #8548. $15–$20

Snoopy wearing red baseball hat, #8546. $20–$25

Junk food series. Determined, 1979.

Snoopy on top of a hamburger sandwich. $18–$28

Snoopy inside a bag of french fries. $15–$25

Snoopy lying on top of a hot dog. $15–$22

Snoopy sitting in front of a chocolate ice cream cone. $15–$25

Snoopy as Santa Claus, with gift sack of toys. Determined, 15″, early 1980s. (Pictured in color insert). $150–$200

GLASS

Snoopy, sitting. "United Feature Syndicate" must be embossed on bottom. Later issue of same bank had paper sticker. Anchor Hocking, #39, 1979. Embossed. $15

PAPIER-MÂCHÉ

Animal series. Determined, mid 1970s.

Snoopy sitting on top of blue chicken, #8441. $20–$25

Snoopy lying on top of gray elephant, #8442. $22–$27

Snoopy sitting on top of white swan, #8443. $22–$27

Assorted (not from a series). Determined, early 1980s.

Snoopy with sunglasses and blue turtleneck sweater, #1516.
$10–$15

Snoopy is wearing a blue warm-up suit and is jogging with Woodstock behind him, #1515. $15–$20

Assorted (not from a series). Determined, mid 1970s.

Woodstock, standing, #1503. $10–$15

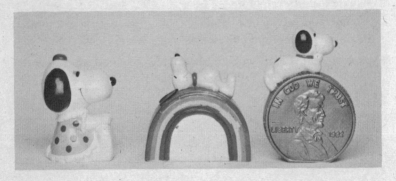

Assorted (not from a series). Determined.

Belle, sitting, wears her famous pink dress, #1500. 1981. $10–$15

Snoopy on top of rainbow, #8533. 1976. $8–$12

Snoopy on top of dime, #1617. Early 1980s. $14–$18

Baseball series. Each character wearing a baseball outfit. Determined, 1973.

Peppermint Patty.	$40–$50
Charlie Brown.	$20–$30
Snoopy.	$20–$30
Lucy.	$35–$45
Linus.	$35–$45
Schroeder.	$40–$50

Doghouse. Snoopy lying on roof of house. This is a Bank of America premium. It is the box only that indicates "Bank of America" on two of its four sides. There is no special marking on the bank itself. Determined for Bank of America, 3¼″ x 6″, early 1970s. $25–$35*

Doghouse. Snoopy lying on roof of house. This is the same bank that was used as a Bank of America premium, but without the Bank of America box there is very little value, as large quantities were sold in the stores over a ten-year period. Determined, #0918, 3¼″ x 6″, 1969.
     $3–$8

Doghouse. Snoopy lying on roof of house. Woodstock is in front of Snoopy's feet. Manufacturer's name on box only. Ideal, 1977.

$30–$45*

Doghouse. Same as above, but version later made by Determined.

$20–$30*

Fruit series. Determined, 1976. (In photo, front row includes first three items, and back row includes last three items.)

Snoopy lying on top of apple. $22–$27

Snoopy lying on top of strawberry. $22–$27

Snoopy lying on top of orange. $20–$25

Snoopy lying on top of lemon with Woodstock on his head.

$16–$21

Snoopy lying on top of slice of watermelon. $16–$21

Snoopy lying on top of banana. $10–$15

Passbook. Snoopy lying on top of passbook savings book. Determined, #8532, 1976.

Gold. $18–$22

Blue. $16–$20

Papier-mâché composition banks. Ideal, 1977.

Snoopy as a fireman, #5298-5. $20–$35*

Snoopy as Joe Cool, orange shirt captioned "Joe Cool," #5255-5.

$20–$35*

Papier-mâché composition banks. Same as above, but version later made by Determined. $15–$20*

Sports ball series. Determined, 1976.

Snoopy lying on baseball, #8531. $12–$17

Snoopy lying on football, #8534. $15–$20

Snoopy lying on soccer ball, #8535.	$12–$17
Snoopy lying on basketball, #8538.	$12–$17
Snoopy lying on bowling ball, #8539.	$22–$27

Transportation series. Determined, 1977. (In photo, front row includes first three items and back row includes last three items.)

Snoopy in red convertible, #8473.	$15–$20
Snoopy in motorboat (yellow deck), #8474.	$12–$17
Snoopy in orange airplane, #8475.	$18–$23
Snoopy in yellow truck, #8476.	$20–$25
Snoopy in green truck, #8476.	$22–$27
Snoopy in blue convertible, #8472.	$18–$23

PLASTIC

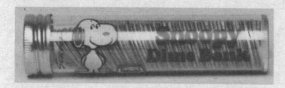

Rival Dog Food dime bank (premium). Cylindrical shape, clear plastic, metal cover, early 1970s. $15–$20

SILVER

Leonard Silver, 1979.

Snoopy, sitting, #9672.	$25–$30
Snoopy pictured with various objects, each representing a letter of the alphabet A–E, cube-shaped, #9669.	$30–$35
Snoopy as a baseball player, #9683.	$40–$50
Snoopy lying atop his doghouse, #9670.	$25–$30*
Woodstock, standing (gold tone), #9673.	$35–$40*

Books,
Comic Books,
and
Records

It seems fitting that the first property to appear outside of the daily syndicated comic strip was a book, even though it was only a compilation of comic strips that had been previously published. For in the ensuing 38 years, 1300 *Peanuts* books have been published in 27 different languages—not to mention a growing literature of books and magazine articles written by or about Charles M. Schulz or dealing with the world of *Peanuts*-related matters.

That first book, simply entitled *Peanuts*, by Charles M. Schulz and published by Rinehart & Co., came out in 1952, barely two years after the strip began. It is particularly instructive to collectors (and historians) who wish to trace the artistic development of the characters in the strip.

As noted previously, our price range encompasses good to mint quality. One other pricing factor influences the value of *Peanuts* books. That is the matter of first editions. Book collectors prize first edition (first printing) books. You will find yourself paying more for a first edition than prices listed here.

Although most publishers identify the edition number in their books, Determined does not. The reason for this is Determined considered its books (including the classic "Happiness Is a Warm Puppy") as products rather than as books. Therefore, if Determined reproduced a book several years later, after its initial printing, it did not see a need to identify the book as a subsequent edition.

A note about pop-up books. Inspect them carefully. They all have working parts. Be sure that all the pages and parts are there and the parts are working properly before you pay top dollar. Pop-up books are a desirable collectible.

BOOKS

Assorted

A Letter From Me. Cover: Charlie Brown reaching to mail a letter. Ambassador, #100HEK 46J, 1972. $4–$8

All About Friendship. Commentary on friends by the *Peanuts* characters. Cover: Snoopy lying on doghouse with Woodstock standing on his tummy. Hallmark, #100HEK 4-3, 1971. $4–$8

All I Want for Christmas Is. . . . Cover: Charlie Brown making out his list. Hallmark, #150XTR 8-4, 1972. $8–$10

The Gospel According to Peanuts, by Robert Short. The author lends a theological interpretation to the *Peanuts* cartoons. John Knox Press, 1964.

    Soft cover. $3–$4

    Hard cover (not shown). $10–$12

Happiness Is a Warm Puppy, by Charles M. Schulz. Cover: Lucy hugging Snoopy. Determined, 1962. Hard cover. $3–$5

It Shouldn't Happen to You . . . Let Alone a Dog. A get well card book. Cover: Snoopy in bed with thermometer. Hallmark, #100HEK 4-15, 1972. $4–$8

Love Sweet Love. Romantic thoughts by the *Peanuts* characters. Cover: Snoopy hugging Charlie Brown. The character Sophie makes a rare appearance in this book. Hallmark, #100HEK 4-6, 1971.
$8–$10

It's Fun to Lie Here and Listen to the Sounds of the Night!, by Charles M. Schulz. Cover: Snoopy lying on top of his doghouse. Determined, 1970. $8–$10

Peanuts, by Charles M. Schulz. Cover: Patty taking picture of Schroeder and Snoopy on piano. A frowning Charlie Brown stands behind. Rinehart & Co., 1952. $4–$8

Peanuts Philosophers, by Charles M. Schulz. Four little books in a cardboard case. Hallmark, 1972. Set. $15–$20

   Linus on Life.

   Snoopy's Philosophy.

   The Wisdom of Charlie Brown.

   The World According to Lucy.

More Peanuts Philosophers, by Charles M. Schulz. Four little books in a cardboard case. Hallmark, 1972. Set. $15–$20

Charlie Brown's Reflections.

Lucy Looks at Life.

The Meditations of Linus.

The Wit and Wisdom of Snoopy.

Peanuts Treasury, by Charles M. Schulz. An anthology of Peanuts cartoons. Holt, Rinehart & Winston, 1968, first edition. $15–$20

Snoopy and the Red Baron, by Charles M. Schulz. Cover: Snoopy as the Flying Ace on roof of his doghouse. Holt, Rinehart & Winston, Canada, 1966, first edition. $4–$6

Snoopy's Secret Code Book, by Charles M. Schulz and Kathryn W. Lumley. Cover: Snoopy with magnifying glass and Sherlock Holmes hat. Used as a teaching aid in the fields of reading, word recognition, and spelling. Rare characters such as Pigpen, Violet, Frieda, Thibault, Jose Peterson, and Franklin are pictured. Holt, Rinehart & Winston, 1971. $12–$15

Winning May Not Be Everything But Losing Isn't Anything, by Charles M. Schulz. Cover: a dejected Charlie Brown with baseball gear. Determined, 1970. $8–$10

The World of Charlie Brown. Out of 14 books which were published at various times between 1959 and 1970, Mattel reprinted one seven-volume collection (two books per volume) and packaged the entire set in its own red cardboard bookcase. Mattel, 1979. $65–$100

Yes Santa, There is a Charlie Brown, by Charles M. Schulz. Hallmark, 1971.

3″ x 4¼″. $7–$10

5″ x 6¾″. $7–$10

Pop-Up Books

Christmas Time With Snoopy and His Friends. Based on the comic strip created by Charles M. Schulz. Cover: Snoopy wearing Santa hat pulling Woodstock on a sled in front of decorated doghouse as Lucy and Charlie Brown look on. Hallmark, #495HEC 80, 1978.

$25–$35

It's Good to Have a Friend, by Charles M. Schulz. Cover: dancing Snoopy and Woodstock. Hallmark, #400HEC 36, 1972. $35–$40

The Peanuts Philosophers, by Charles M. Schulz. Cover: Lucy in "medical advice" booth, Snoopy in booth captioned: "Hug a Warm Puppy 1¢." Woodstock is flying upside down. Hallmark, #400HEC 33, 1972. $35–$45

Love à La Peanuts, by Charles M. Schulz. Cover: Lucy kneels on piano as she gives Schroeder a kiss. Hallmark, #400HEC 35, 1972.

$35–$45

Pop-up page from *Love à La Peanuts.*

Snoopy's Secret Life, by Charles M. Schulz. Cover: Snoopy as the Flying Ace sits on his doghouse. Hallmark, #400CHE C34, 1972.

$30–$40

COMIC BOOKS

Nancy. Cover: Sluggo polishing Nancy's toenails. *Peanuts* cartoons inside not signed by Schulz. Dell, #146, September 1957. $8–$15

Nancy and Sluggo. Cover: Sluggo giving Nancy a hotdog. *Peanuts* cartoons inside not signed by Schulz. Dell, #177, July–August 1960. $5–$12

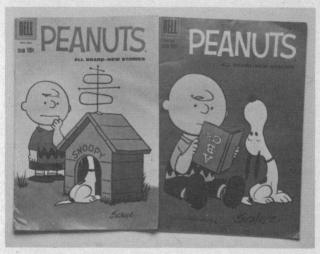

Peanuts. Cover: Charlie Brown looking at Snoopy who is in his house watching television. Cover signed by Schulz. Inside cartoons are not. This book also has one story featuring Sluggo. Dell, #5, May–July 1960. $20–$25

Peanuts. Cover: Charlie Brown sitting and reading "ABC" book upside down. Snoopy sitting next to him is looking up to sky. Cover signed by Schulz but cartoons inside are not. There are no non-*Peanuts* stories in this edition. Dell, #969, 1959. $20–$30

MIB (Mint In Box): Item in unopened box, box in excellent condition.

Mint Condition: Superior quality, box missing.

Good Condition: All parts are included. Item and/or box shows limited wear and tear.

Poor Condition: Major wear and tear. Parts may be missing.

Tip Top. Cover: Charlie Brown, Lucy, Schroeder, Snoopy in baseball scene. Nancy and Sluggo appear over title. No artist signature. The *Peanuts* strip inside credits Charles M. Schulz but again his signature does not appear. United Feature, #187, July–August 1954.

$25–$40

Peanuts. Cover: Charlie Brown and Snoopy watching television. Signed by Schulz. Inside cartoons do not bear any signature. Dell, #878, 1958.

$20–$30

RECORDS

Good Grief, Charlie Brown! Peanuts. Kay Ballard as Lucy and Arthur Siegel as Charlie Brown deliver a series of sketches mostly dealing with Charlie Brown's insecurities. Cover: Lucy and Charlie Brown who asks, "Kay Ballard and Arthur Siegel?" Columbia Records, #HS 11230 HL 7430, late 1960s.

$25–$35

Oh Good Grief, Vince Guaraldi. Jazz music from *Peanuts* television specials. Cover: Schroeder at the piano. Snoopy with mustache and glasses. Warner Bros., #1747, 1968.

$10–$15

A Boy Named Charlie Brown. Rod McKuen performs and conducts all his songs from this album. Cover: A four-panel cartoon featuring Sally telling Charlie Brown she was sent to the principal's office at school because she couldn't draw a cow's leg and that Rod McKuen probably can't draw one either. Charlie Brown asks, "Rod Mc-Kuen?" Stanyon Records, #SR 5010, 1970.   *$20–$30*

You're a Good Man, Charlie Brown. Original TV cast album. Hallmark Hall of Fame. Cover: Patty, Linus, Snoopy, Schroeder, and Lucy lift Charlie Brown who wears a crown. Cover also has sticker, "On National TV February 9, 1973." Atlantic Records, #SD 7252, 1972.
                                                          $25–$35

An asterisk (*) next to a price indicates that the item comes with its original box in excellent condition. If no asterisk is shown, there is no box or the box adds little significant value. Shipping boxes (no graphics) are of no value.

A copyright date indicates the year the character first appeared in a particular incarnation, *not* the year the product first came out.

Ceramic Bells and Plates

Some of the most creative and collectible work to go into any *Peanuts* objects will be found in the ceramic plates and bells, most of which were crafted by Schmid.

This will be one of the few chapters in the book where items that came out beyond the early 1980s will appear. Since Schmid gave up its license in 1986, we felt it would make sense to include the last few years of Schmid plate and bell production. This will enable the reader to have reference to the entire Schmid collection in one volume.

For the serious collectors, we are including a discussion of the dating and nomenclature of Schmid's plates and bells. It gets a little bit tricky but it is not necessary to memorize it. You might just want to keep this around as a reference. Here goes.

For awhile Schmid annually came out with plates on three occasions: Valentine's Day, Mother's Day, and Christmas. They also came out with a Mother's Day bell each year since 1974 and a Christmas bell each year since 1973—with the exception of 1974 when there was no Christmas bell. All of these items were "dated." Except for the face bells, the bell and plate of each particular year share a similar design theme.

There came a point in time when Schmid decided to produce only one plate each year instead of three and only one bell each year instead of two. (There were never any Valentine's Day bells.) These "single" entries became known as "annuals," since there then became only *one plate and bell annually*.

For the plates, the "annual" production of only one plate began in 1983 and continued through 1986. The bells were put into "annual" status much earlier, in 1979. That, too, lasted until the series ended in 1986.

Got it so far? Good. Here comes the tricky part.

In 1979 and 1983 Schmid did a couple of things to trip us up. In 1979 when they converted the bells to an "annual" basis they alternated the celebration of Mother's Day and Christmas—1979 was a Mother's Day bell, 1980 was a Christmas bell, 1981 Mother's Day, and 1982 Christmas. Then came 1983 and Schmid deemed that, just as in music boxes, the annual plates and bells would no longer be in celebration of either holiday, Mother's Day or Christmas. Instead they chose a general theme, such as "In Concert" in 1983. But Schmid took the plates one step further. Schmid limited the production of plates in 1983 to 15,000 and called the 1983 plates the "First Annual Limited Edition." This continued through the "Fourth Annual Limited Edition," the "Flyin' Tamer Snoopy" plates of 1986, when it all ended. These became known as "Annual Limited Editions."

Unfortunately for us, they treated the bells slightly different. Although the design treatment for the bells also went to a general theme in 1983, Schmid did not make them "limited editions" until 1985. Thus the bells only had two limited editions, the "first" in 1985 and the "second" in 1986—the plates, although they had the same theme, had limited editions for four years.

And for good measure, Schmid added one other feature to the bells in 1985. They made the handles figural—Snoopy with his friend Woodstock in 1985 and Snoopy alone in 1986.

In each and every case—the dated, the annual, and the annual limited editions—the themes and poses closely resembled those of the music boxes.

Now that wasn't too bad, was it? In our opinion the beauty of the ceramic plates and bells makes the whole exercise worthwhile.

BELLS

Annuals

1983, *Peanuts in Concert.* Snoopy and the gang in band costumes, each playing a different instrument. Caption around rim: "Peanuts in Concert. 1983." Schmid. $20–$30*

1984, *Snoopy and the Beaglescouts.* Characters in scout outfits out hiking. Production limited to 10,000. Schmid. $20–$30*

1985, *Clown Capers.* The gang is dressed in clown costumes. Linus is cranking up the car. This was Schmid's first *Peanuts* bell with a figure as the handle (Snoopy and Woodstock). Also known as the First Limited Edition Bell. Schmid. $20–$30*

1986, *Flyin' Tamer Snoopy.* Snoopy pretends to be a lion tamer and Woodstock is the lion. Snoopy figure is the handle. Also known as the Second Limited Edition Bell. Schmid. $20–$30*

Bicentennial

1976. Snoopy is lying on top of Liberty Bell. Caption: "1776–1976." Schmid. $25–$30*

Christmas

1973. Snoopy wearing stocking cap is on top of his doghouse. Stockings decorate his house. Woodstock is on top of tree that is next to Snoopy's house. Schmid. $40–$60*

1975. Snoopy is on top of his house. Woodstock, wearing Santa outfit, is standing on Snoopy's nose. Schmid. $25–$35*

1976. Snoopy is looking at Woodstock who has a tree in his nest. Schmid. $25–$35*

1977. Snoopy is lying on top of his house which is covered with different colored lights. Schmid. $25–$35*

1978. Snoopy as Santa with bag of goodies is standing in front of fireplace. Woodstock is inside one of the stockings. Schmid.
$25–$35*

1980. Snoopy looking at tree hung with stockings. Woodstock is in nest in tree. Schmid. $35–$45*

1982. Snoopy is ice skating. "Perfect Performance" is printed inside bell. Schmid. $25–$35*

Face Bells

Schmid, 6″, 1974.

Lucy, #278-417.	$35–$50
Schroeder, #278-419.	$40–$55
Snoopy, #278-415.	$30–$45
Linus, #278-418.	$35–$50
Snoopy as the Flying Ace, #278-415.	$40–$55
Charlie Brown, #278-416.	$40–$55

Mother's Day

1977. Snoopy is on his doghouse typing the words "Dear Mom." Schmid. $20–$25*

1978. Snoopy and Woodstock each have a rose. Snoopy thinking "Mom," Woodstock chirping "iiii." Schmid. $20–$25*

1979. Snoopy is typing the words "Dear Mom." The "o" is his paw print. Schmid. $20–$25*

1981. "Mission For Mom" printed inside bell. Snoopy as the Flying Ace is on his doghouse. Clouds form "MOM." Schmid. $20–$25*

PLATES

Anniversary

Happy Anniversary 1950–1980. Snoopy on his house as Flying Ace, Spike in the desert, Woodstock in his nest, Sally reading, Marcie, Peppermint Patty, Linus with blanket, Schroeder at piano with Lucy leaning on it, and Franklin. Schmid. $45–$50*

Annuals

1983, Peanuts in Concert. First limited edition. Production limited to 20,000. Snoopy conducts the band using Schroeder's piano as a podium while Woodstock sits on a bar of music. Members of the band include Lucy, Linus, Sally, and Charlie Brown. Schmid. $25–$30*

1984, Snoopy and the Beaglescouts. Second limited edition. Production limited to 20,000. Scoutmaster Snoopy leads Woodstock and the Beaglescouts on a hike. Schmid. $25–$35*

1985, Clown Capers. Third limited edition. Production limited to 20,000. The gang, dressed in clown costumes, happily watches Linus crank up their colorful old car. Inside the car are Peppermint Patty, Schroeder, Franklin, Marcie, Sally, and Charlie Brown. Lucy stands outside while Snoopy lies on the back bar and Woodstock stands on hood in front of driver. Schmid. $25–$35*

1986, Flyin' Tamer Snoopy. Fourth limited edition. Production limited to 20,000. Snoopy acts as lion tamer as Woodstock pretends to be the lion. Schmid. $25–$30*

Athletic

Football. One of four plates from the World's Greatest Athlete collection. Titled: "Go Deep." Snoopy and Woodstock with football in the air. Limited to 10,000. Numbered. Schmid, 1983. $40–$45*

Ice Hockey. One of four plates from the World's Greatest Athlete collection. Titled: "The Puck Stops Here." Snoopy and Woodstock trying to hit the puck. Limited to 10,000. Numbered. Schmid, 1983.   *$40–$45**

Tennis. One of four plates from the World's Greatest Athlete collection. Titled: "The Way You Play the Game." Snoopy with tennis racket raised, ready to hit the ball. Limited to 10,000. Numbered. Schmid, 1983.   *$40–$45**

Baseball. One of four plates from the World's Greatest Athlete collection. Titled: "The Crowd Went Wild." Snoopy with baseball bat, "POW." Schmid, 1983.   *$40–$45**

Bicentennial

1976. Snoopy lying on top of Liberty Bell. Caption: "1776–1976." Schmid, 1976.   *$25–$35**

Birthday

"Happy Birthday" captioned on plate. Snoopy and Woodstock with balloons in center. Encircling plate are train cars carrying Linus, Schroeder, Charlie Brown, Peppermint Patty, Woodstock, and Snoopy. Determined for the Dupont Collection Ltd., mid 1970s.

$25–$30*

Christmas Dated

1972, *Snoopy Guides the Sleigh.* Snoopy in sleigh, Woodstock at end of reins. Schmid. $30–$50*

1973, *Christmas Eve at the Doghouse.* Snoopy, wearing stocking cap, is on top of his doghouse. Stockings decorate his house. Woodstock is on top of tree that is next to Snoopy's house. Schmid. $100–$200*

1974, *Christmas Eve at the Fireplace.* Snoopy is in front of fireplace lying on some gifts. Woodstock is lying on a gift. Stockings hang on fireplace. Schmid. $45–$65*

1975, *Woodstock, Santa Claus.* Snoopy is on top of his house. Woodstock, wearing Santa outfit, is standing on Snoopy's nose. Schmid. $20–$30*

1976, *Woodstock's Christmas.* Snoopy looking at Woodstock who has a tree in his nest. Schmid. $20–$25*

1977, *Deck the Doghouse.* Snoopy is lying on top of his house which is covered with different colored lights. Schmid. $20–$25*

1978, *Filling the Stockings.* Snoopy as Santa with bag of goodies is standing in front of fireplace. Woodstock is inside one of the Christmas stockings. Schmid. $25–$30*

1979, *Christmas at Hand.* Snoopy is standing on the roof of his house doing his pawpet act. Schmid. $20–$25*

1980, *Waiting for Santa.* Snoopy looking at tree hung with stockings. Woodstock is in nest in tree. Schmid. $40–$60*

1981, *A Christmas Wish.* Snoopy on his house covered with different colored stockings. Production limited to 15,000. Schmid. $20–$25*

1982, *Perfect Performance.* Snoopy writes "Merry" on the ice with his feet which also serve as skates. Schmid. $45–$55*

Christmas Undated

"*Merry Christmas*" *captioned on plate.* Tree is being trimmed by Woodstocks. Lucy, Charlie Brown, Linus, Peppermint Patty, and Schroeder look like elves with toys. Snoopy is doing his pawpet act. Determined, mid-1970s. $25–$30*

Mother's Day

1972, Linus. Linus holds a rose. Schmid. $15–$20*

1973, Mom. Snoopy is looking at Woodstock who is holding a sign which reads "MOM?" Schmid. $15–$20*

1974, Snoopy and Woodstock on Parade. Snoopy is holding a banner with a heart on it. Woodstock is walking behind him with "Mom" banner. Schmid. $20–$30*

1975, A Kiss For Lucy. Snoopy is giving Lucy a kiss on the cheek. Schmid. $20–$25*

1976, Linus and Snoopy. Snoopy, Woodstock, and Linus are each holding a flower. Schmid. $20–$25*

1977, Dear Mom. Snoopy is on his house typing "Dear Mom." Schmid. $20–$25*

1978, Thoughts That Count. Snoopy and Woodstock each have a rose. Snoopy saying "Mom," Woodstock saying "iiii." Schmid.
$20–$25*

1979, A Special Letter. Snoopy is typing "Dear Mom." The "o" is his pawprint. Production limited to 10,000. Schmid. $20–$25*

1980, A Tribute to Mom. On the front of the plate there is a big word, "MOM," with Snoopy coming out of the "O." Woodstock in front holding flowers. Production limited to 10,000. Schmid. $35–$40*

1981, *Mission For Mom.* Snoopy as the Flying Ace is on his doghouse. Clouds form "MOM." Schmid. $25–$30*

1982, *Which Way to Mother.* Snoopy and Woodstock are in front of a directional sign with "Mom" written in various languages. Schmid. $25–$30*

Valentine's Day

1977, *Home is Where the Heart Is.* Snoopy is on top of a red and white gingham heart with lace trim. Schmid. $15–$20*

1978, *Heavenly Bliss.* Snoopy is under a red umbrella as it rains hearts. Schmid. $20–$25*

1979, *Love Match.* Snoopy is playing tennis and a heart comes at him instead of a tennis ball. Schmid. $20–$30*

1980, *From Snoopy With Love.* Snoopy is blowing pink bubble hearts as Woodstock watches. Schmid. $20–$25*

1981, *Hearts-a-Flutter.* Charlie Brown is running with a heart-shaped kite. Snoopy is watching from the background. Schmid. $35–$40*

1982, *Love Patch.* Snoopy as a scarecrow in a field of hearts. Schmid. $20–$25*

Decorative Items

The memorabilia in the various sections of this chapter have two things in common. They all make nice gifts and most of them are utilitarian. People who originally bought them were able to justify the expenditures to themselves because they were buying things they could use and/or which would enhance the ambiance of their homes.

Of course, few people who purchased the Crystal Snoopy by Determined way back in 1972 would have dared to justify this particular purchase as an investment. But that is just what happened as this unheralded—and not overly produced—piece of workmanship became the darling of collectors and skyrocketed from an original selling price of $29.95 all the way to today's market value of $150–$200.

The mirror pictures, also a favorite of many collectors, were made in England and distributed in the United States by Determined.

With the exception of the pieces by Oden listed in the "Stained Glass" section, most of what we call stained glass really isn't. The glass is colored either by a silk-screen or a handpainted process.

BANNERS

"All Systems Are Go!" Snoopy attired in astronaut gear. Determined, 1970. $15–$20

"For a Nickel I Can Cure Anything." Lucy in her psychiatrist booth. Determined, 1971. $6–$10

"Happiness Is Loving Your Enemies." Snoopy and the bunnies. Determined, 1970 (above left). $20–$25

"Merry Christmas From All of Us." Sally, Charlie Brown, Violet, Schroeder, Lucy, Linus, Snoopy. Determined, early 1970s (above right). $20–$30

I Am Suddenly Overcome by a Burst of Wishy Washiness." Charlie Brown. Determined, early 1970s. $10–$12

"I Don't Need Any Downs! I Want 'Ups' and 'Ups'!" Lucy. Determined, early 1970s. $10–$15

"The Moon Is Made of American Cheese." Snoopy. Determined, 1970. $10–$15

CERAMIC EGGS

Aviva, #199, 1972 originally. (Photo includes last four items.)

Snoopy holding a supper dish and grinning. Thought balloon: "I'm So Cute." $8-$10

Snoopy holding a supper dish and grinning. Thought balloon: "I'm So Cute." Framed by an oval. $8-$10

Snoopy as a chef. Caption: "Joe Gourmet." $8-$10

Snoopy is on the roof of his house. Musical notes are coming out of his door. Caption: "Security Is a Happy Home." $8-$10

Snoopy is kissing Lucy. Caption: "SMAK." $8-$10

Snoopy is wearing a scout hat with lots of Woodstocks on the brim. Caption: "World's Greatest Dad." $8-$10

Snoopy leaping. Caption: "World's Greatest Mom." $8-$10

CHRISTMAS ITEMS

Peanuts collector tile. Caption: "Merry Christmas 1978." Snoopy is reading a list captioned "Good Boys & Girls." A sleigh is filled with gifts and Woodstocks. Determined, 5¾" x 5¾", 1978. $25-$35*

Wreath, ceramic. Snoopy hugging Woodstock on top of the wreath. Snoopy wears a red Santa hat trimmed with white. Determined, 12" diam., early 1980s. (Pictured in color insert.) $150-$175

Wreath, ceramic. Snoopy hugging Woodstock on top of the wreath. A large, red bow highlights the top portion of the wreath for both large and smaller ceramic wreaths. Determined, 5″ diam., early 1980s. (Pictured in color insert.) $35–$45

CRYSTAL AND SILVER

Crystal sitting Snoopy. Bottom etched "United Feature Syndicate 1972." Determined, 1972. $150–$200

Silver Snoopy heart box. Snoopy sits on top of lid. Caption on lid: "Love." Red velvet lined. Leonard Silver, 1979. $20–$25

GRAPHIC PRINTS

Aviva, 16″x 20″, 1981.
    Snoopy with a tennis racket. Thought balloon: "Out?!!" $20–$30
    Snoopy as Joe Cool standing by school lockers. $20–$30
    Snoopy as the Flying Ace sits on a pastel-colored rainbow.
                                              $20–$30

Snoopy sleeping against a tree as Woodstock sleeps in his nest.
                                        $20–$30

Snoopy is lying on Charlie Brown's head as they watch television. $20–$30

MIRROR PICTURES

Snoopy, Woodstocks, Linus, Schroeder, Lucy, Peppermint Patty, Charlie Brown and Sally. They're in and near a London double-decker bus. Determined, 13¼" x 9¼", mid 1970s. $25–$35

Snoopy as the Flying Ace. Snoopy sits on the roof of his house. Determined, 9" x 13¼", mid 1970s. $20–$25

Peppermint Patty holds hands with Charlie Brown. Snoopy is hugging Woodstock. Large hearts appear in background. Caption: "Love." Determined, 10½" x 8", mid 1970s. $25–$30

Snoopy is in an air balloon. Woodstocks fly all around. Determined, 8" x 10½", mid 1970s. $20–$25

Snoopy, looking very self-satisfied, is thinking "I'm So Cute." Determined, 9¼" x 13¼", mid 1970s. $20–$25

Snoopy holds a large group of balloons. Woodstock holds a red balloon that says "Love." Determined, 9″ x 12¾″, mid 1970s.

$25–$30

Snoopy, sitting. Caption: "Start Each Day With a Smile." Determined, 13¼″ x 9¼″, mid 1970s. $20–$25

Snoopy dressed in formal attire. Determined, 12″ x 18″, mid 1970s. $65–$75

MOBILES AND WINDCHIMES

Peanuts musical mobile. Charlie Brown, Linus, Lucy, Sally, Snoopy, and Woodstock. Wood. Nursery Originals, #231–800, 1980.

$35–$45*

PEANUTS MOBILE

Peanuts mobile. Charlie Brown, Linus, Lucy, Schroeder, and Snoopy, who is on his doghouse. There is a big orange sunburst, pink cloud, and large green cloud. This stiff, glossy cardboard mobile is packaged on a punchout cardboard. Determined, 1973.

Small, 8¾″ x 12″.	$15–$20*
Large, 18″ x 24″.	$30–$35*

Windchime. Snoopy wearing headphones and roller skates. Accompanied by Woodstock. Ceramic. Several musical notes complete the design. Came in a variety of color combinations. Quantasia, #124001, 1984. $15–$25

Windchime. Snoopy is lying on his house surrounded by a green lawn. Plastic with metal windchimes. A plastic Woodstock acts as a weight. Aviva, 1973. $20–$30*

NEEDLECRAFT KITS

Crewel. Caption: "No One Understands My Generation." Snoopy stands outside Lucy's psychiatrist booth. Woodstock sits on top of the booth. Malina, #8110–018, 12″ x 16″, mid 1970s. $8–$15*

Crewel. Caption: "To Know Me Is to Love Me." Snoopy and Charlie Brown looking pleased with each other. Malina, #8110–016, 8″ x 10″, mid 1970s. $8–$12*

Felt. Four jeweled hanging ornaments featuring Snoopy. Malina, #8400/002 "Snoopy," late 1970s. $25–$35*

Felt. Jeweled Christmas stocking kit. Snoopy is typing a "Dear Santa" list while Woodstock looks on. Malina, #8450/001 "My List," 18″ diag., late 1970s. $18–$25*

Felt. Jeweled Christmas stocking (finished product). Snoopy forms a snowman as Woodstock sits on its head. Malina, #8450/003 "Snow Pals," 18″ diag., late 1970s. $18–$25*

Felt. Jeweled Christmas panel. Snoopy and Woodstock standing on Snoopy's doghouse exchanging gifts. Malina, #8350/001 "Goodwill," late 1970s. (See color insert.) $25–$35*

MIB (Mint In Box): Item in unopened box, box in excellent condition.

Mint Condition: Superior quality, box missing.

Good Condition: All parts are included. Item and/or box shows limited wear and tear.

Poor Condition: Major wear and tear. Parts may be missing.

Latch hook. Snoopy hugging Woodstock. Malina, #26/13 "Buddies," 20″ x 27″, mid 1970s. $30–$40*

Latch hook. Snoopy as the Flying Ace (head portion only) can be completed into a pillow or wall hanging. Malina, #33/1, 15″ x 15″, mid 1970s. $20–$25*

Quickpoint. Snoopy and Woodstock sitting and laughing. Determined, #4111, 18″ x 18″, 1972. $30–$40*

PATCHES

Determined, 3″ diam., 1970. (Photo includes last three items.)

Snoopy with skis and ski cap. Caption: "To the Bunny Slope." #730. $3–$4*

Snoopy on roller skates. Caption: "Jamming." #731. $3–$4*

Snoopy on his house as the Flying Ace. Caption: "Curse You Red Baron." #726. $3–$4*

Lucy. Caption: "World's Crabbiest Female." #727. $5–$6*

Snoopy. Caption: "Raw Strength and Courage." #722. $3–$4*

Snoopy holding Uncle Sam hat. Caption: "America You're Beautiful." #743. $6–$8*

PICTURE FRAMES

Snoopy lies on top of the frame. Frame is designed to use his name, "S N O O P Y." The pictures go inside the "Os." Enameled. Butterfly, #3935, 7" x 3", 1979. $15–$25

Snoopy is lying on his doghouse. Doghouse holds picture. Enameled. Butterfly, #3921, 2" x 3½", 1979. $10–$15

Snoopy and Woodstock with tennis rackets. Woodstock is "Top Seeded." Enameled. Butterfly, #3922, 3½" x 3¼", 1979. $10–$15

Snoopy and Woodstock. They wear party hats and hold three balloons with cutouts to hold the pictures. Enameled. Butterfly, #3925, 3" x 4½", 1979. $15–$20

Snoopy holding a small pink heart. A larger red-and-pink-trimmed heart holds the picture. Enameled. Butterfly, 3½" x 3¼", 1979.
$15–$20

Snoopy hugging Woodstock. This is depicted on the cover of the compact, which holds two photos. Metal. Butterfly, #1000PP3051, early 1980s. $15–$20

Snoopy stands next to Lucy's psychiatrist booth. Booth holds the picture and is captioned "Friendly Advice 7¢ . . . Your Friend Is Always In." Die-cast. Gun metal gray. Burnes of Boston, early 1980s.
$20–$30

Snoopy stands next to a star-shaped frame. Caption: "A Real Star." Gun metal gray. Die-cast. Burnes of Boston, early 1980s. $20–$30

PLAQUES

Manufacturer unknown. Character plaques. Three-dimensional framed plastic. 8″ x 14″, late 1960s.

Snoopy.	$25–$40
Charlie Brown.	$25–$40
Linus.	$25–$40
Lucy.	$25–$40

Snoopy is being hugged by Charlie Brown. Thought balloon: "The Only Way to Have a Friend Is to Be One." Hallmark plaquette, #135AWB985–6, 3¼″ x 4½″, 1972. $6–$8

Snoopy is lying on his tummy in the grass. Thought balloon: "Work Is the Crab Grass In the Lawn of Life." Cloth covered. Hallmark plaquette #125AWB985–1, 3¼″ x 4½″, 1972. $6–$8

Snoopy lying on top of his house. Thought balloon: "Someday I Must Give Up This Mad Carefree Existence." Hallmark plaquette, #125AWB985–5, 3¼″ x 4½″, 1972. $6–$8

Snoopy sits on his house, shaking his fist. Thought balloon: "Curse You, Red Baron!" Three-dimensional plastic in a white frame. Hallmark, 9″ x 10¾″, late 1960s. $30–$40

Charlie Brown is sitting on a chair. Caption: "I've Developed a New Philosophy . . . I Only Dread One Day at a Time." Three–dimensional plastic in a white frame, Hallmark, 9″ x 10¾″, late 1960s.
                    $30–$40

Schroeder is playing the piano. Lucy looks at him thinking, "It's Amazing How Stupid You Can Be When You're In Love." Hallmark, #DE 4007, 3½″ x 3½″, 1981. $8–$10

Snoopy is hugged by Charlie Brown. Caption: "Have You Hugged Your Dog Today?" Hallmark, #DE 8053, 3″ x 4½″, mid 1970s.
                    $8–$12

Snoopy and Woodstock. They are wearing tall hats and sitting on Snoopy's doghouse, which is decorated with a wreath. Caption: "Christmas Is For Sharing." Iridescent glass with wood frame and stand. Hallmark, 3½″ x 5¼″, 1980. $20–$25

Snoopy and Woodstock are dancing. Snoopy's thought balloon: "Start Each Day With a Smile on Your Lips and a Song in Your Heart." Springbok, 5¾″ x 6″, 1972. $8–$12

Snoopy is kissing Peppermint Patty. Snoopy's thought balloon: "We All Need Someone to Kiss Away Our Tears." Springbok, #400DE113, 5″ x 6″, 1972. $10–$15

Snoopy is being hugged by Charlie Brown. Caption: "Happiness is Having a Friend. . . ." Springbok, #400DE111, 5″ x 7″, 1971.
                    $8–$12

"STAINED GLASS"

Glass

Framed "stained glass." Framed "stained" glass is set ¼″ in front of the backdrop, adding to the illusion of depth and giving it a shadowbox effect. This method gives the illusion of stained glass. Production limited to one year. Aviva, 5½″ x 7½″, 1983 (see photo on previous page, bottom).

Snoopy on his house. Woodstock lying on Snoopy's tummy. Rainbow in the background. Captioned: "Home Sweet Home."

$20–$25

Snoopy picking flowers. Captioned: "Hearts & Flowers."

$20–$25

Snoopy as a cowboy with a lariat. Woodstock as an Indian sitting on a cactus. Captioned: "Happy Trails." $20–$25

Snoopy as a cook. Captioned: "Joe Gourmet." $20–$25

Partially painted window hanging. Gives the illusion of stained glass. Aviva, 5″ x 7″, 1981.

Snoopy as Joe Cool. Captioned: "Joe Cool." $20–$25

Snoopy on his house as the Flying Ace. $20–$25

Snoopy as a chef, commonly known as Joe Gourmet. $20–$25

Snoopy and Woodstock with balloons. $25–$30

Leaded Stained Glass

Snoopy as the Flying Ace, Oden, 1980 $25–$30

Snoopy lies on his house. Woodstock lying on Snoopy's tummy. Oden, 6¾″ l., 1980. $30–$35

Snoopy sitting next to his supper dish. Woodstock in the dish. Oden, 1980. $28–$32

Snoopy sitting. Woodstock behind him. Oden, 1980. $28–$32

Snoopy lies on his tummy on top of a large red heart. Oden, 1980.

$30–$35

Snoopy, sitting, 5½". Oden, 1980. $22–$25

Snoopy, sitting, 4¾". Oden, 1980. $18–$22

Snoopy sitting, holding a red heart, 5½". Oden, 1980. $30–$35

Snoopy sitting holding a red heart, 3½". Oden, 1980. $25–$30

Snoopy with a yellow parachute. Oden, 8½", 1980. $30–$38

Snoopy as Joe Cool. Oden, 4½", 1980. $20–$25

Snoopy on a quarter moon. Oden, 1980. $35–$45

Snoopy dancing. 1980. $20–$25

Plastic

Snoopy on top of red heart. Woodstock on Snoopy's tummy. (Known as Snoopy Sunshiners.) Aviva, late 1970s. $12–$15*

An asterisk (*) next to a price indicates that the item comes with its original box in excellent condition. If no asterisk is shown, there is no box or the box adds little significant value. Shipping boxes (no graphics) are of no value.

_____

A copyright date indicates the year the character first appeared in a particular incarnation, not the year the product first came out.

Snoopy leaning against tree. Woodstock in a nest in the tree. (Known as Snoopy Sunshiners.) Aviva, late 1970s. $12–$15*

Snoopy and Woodstock as Joe Cools, leaning up against school locker. (Known as Snoopy Sunshiners.) Aviva, late 1970s.

$12–$15*

Snoopy as the Flying Ace. Two Woodstocks parachuting. (Known as Snoopy Sunshiners.) Aviva, late 1970s. $12–$15*

Snoopy lying on his tummy on a rainbow. Woodstock is sitting on Snoopy's fanny. (Known as Snoopy Sunshiners.) Aviva, late 1970s.

$12–$15*

Desk Accessories

Three cheers for *Peanuts* desk accessories. They provide a fine opportunity to bring *Peanuts* into the office. As one wit recently observed: "If you are stressed enough to throw your paperweight, don't. Just look at it." It is the wonder of Snoopy that he can bring a smile to your face even on a stressful day.

Speaking of paperweights, you will want to pay particular attention to the etched paperweights by Butterfly. In our opinion they have to be among the most elegant of all paperweights.

In the bookend department, the design of Snoopy kicking a door as he holds his supper dish in his mouth is a classic pose. It is noteworthy, however, that most of his door kicking appears in the comic strips. It is extremely rare for this pose to be found in a figural piece.

BOOKENDS

Ceramic

Snoopy, sitting, as the Flying Ace. He wears a blue helmet and red scarf. Butterfly, #1000 CPE 002, 5″, 1979. $35–$45*

Snoopy, sitting. Wears a yellow slicker and hat. Butterfly, 5″, 1979.
                                                                $35–$45*

Snoopy, sitting. Dressed as a tennis player. Butterfly, #1000 1301, 5″, 1979. $30–$40*

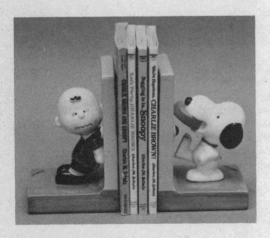

Charlie Brown leaning up against door. Opposite bookend: Snoopy, kicking orange door with his foot. Holds supper dish in his mouth. Butterfly, mid 1970s. $60–$80*

Rubber

Snoopy, sitting and hugging Woodstock. Heart-shaped red hard rubber. Butterfly, #700 1303, 1981. $18–$22*

BULLETIN BOARDS

Cork

Map of the United States. Decorated with Snoopy, Woodstocks, and Belle. Colorful. Manton Cork Co., 35″ x 23″, 1983. $15–$30*

Metal

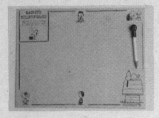

Magnetic board. Pictures (clockwise) of Lucy, Schroeder, and Snoopy at the piano, Snoopy on his doghouse, Linus, and Sally. Charlie Brown and Snoopy are in inset. Color: blue. Simon Simple, 12″ x 9″, late 1960s. $15–$25

Magnetic board. Pictures (clockwise) of Snoopy and a bunny, Linus and Lucy, Snoopy on his doghouse, Charlie Brown flying a kite, Lucy with balloon, Snoopy and Schroeder at the piano, and Charlie Brown with Snoopy. Color: white. Simon Simple, 18″ x 14″, late 1960s. $25–$40

MISCELLANEOUS DESK ACCESSORIES

Autograph book. Cover depicts Linus with a camera, Snoopy as a director, sitting in his director's chair wearing a beret and dark glasses, Charlie Brown in baseball gear on the mound, and Lucy in baseball gear, who are the stars of the movie *A Boy Named Charlie Brown.* This caption appears on the cover. A & M Leatherlines, Inc., 1971. $15–$25

Desk blotter with accessories. Note pad and holder, pen and holder, large address book. Butterfly, early 1980s. $30–$45

Glue in plastic bottle. Duro (Woodhill Chemical Sales Corp.), early 1970s.

Charlie Brown in baseball gear, white glue, 4 oz. $12–$15

Charlie Brown is wearing a baseball hat, school glue, 4 oz.
                                                      $12–$15

Flying Ace, Snoopy, white glue, 4 oz. $12–$15

Flying Ace, Snoopy, school glue, 4 oz. $12–$15

Linus with his blanket and thumb in his mouth, 4 oz. $12–$15

Linus smiling, school glue, 2 oz. $10–$12

Letter holder. Oval-shaped. Four related pictures and thoughts of Snoopy decorate this red, white, and black metal letter holder. One picture shows Snoopy on his house as the Flying Ace. Thought balloon: "Here's the World War I Flying Ace Searching for the Red Baron . . ." A & M Leatherlines, Inc., late 1960s. $10–$20

Letter holder. Orange, black, and oval-shaped. The gang includes Sally, Schroeder, Violet, Snoopy, Pigpen, Frieda, Linus, Lucy, and Charlie Brown. Captioned: "The In Crowd." Metal. A & M Leatherlines, Inc., late 1960s. $10–$20

Note pad. Chunky white with black and red drawings. Cover: Snoopy on his house as the Flying Ace. Thought balloon: "Here's the WWI Flying Ace Zooming Through the Air in His Sopwith Camel." A & M Leatherlines, Inc., 1971. $6–$10

Pencil cup. Black and red drawings. Snoopy on his house as the Flying Ace. Thought balloon: "Curse You Red Baron." A & M Leatherlines, Inc., 1971. $8–$12

Peanuts Desk Set. Linus decorates the top of the stapler, Charlie Brown, in his baseball hat, is the tape dispenser, and Snoopy, lying on a mailbox, becomes the letter opener. Springbok, #DSK 1201, early 1970s. $45–$65*

PAPERWEIGHTS

Ceramic

Snoopy, Woodstock. Sits in red supper dish. Butterfly, #300CP PW004, 3½", mid 1970s. $15–$25*

Snoopy. Sits at his yellow and blue typewriter on heart-shaped base. Butterfly, #300CP PW003, 3½", mid 1970s. $15–$25*

Snoopy. Wears a red cap and backpack, leans against a rock, Butterfly, #300CP PW005, 3½", mid 1970s. $15–$25*

Snoopy. Sits in a pale green easy chair. Butterfly, #300CP PW002, 3½", mid 1970s. $15–$25*

Snoopy. Sits on a yellow base wearing a red baseball hat and holding a blue bat. Butterfly, #300CP PW001, 3½", mid 1970s. $15–$25*

Snoopy as Joe Cool. Lies on his back with head against rock. He is wearing a red shirt and green shades. Butterfly, #1008, 3½", 1979.

$8-$10*

Snoopy. Lies on his tummy. Butterfly, #1007, 4¼", 1979. $10-$12*

Snoopy. Sits and hugs Woodstock. Butterfly, #1009, 1979.

$10-$12*

Snoopy. Lies on his back. Butterfly, #1005, 1979. $10-$12*

Snoopy. Lies on his tummy leaning on his paws. Butterfly, #1004, 1979. $10-$12*

Snoopy as the Flying Ace. Wears a blue helmet with black goggles on it, and is sitting and hugging Woodstock. Butterfly, #1023, 1979. $12-$14*

Snoopy. Sits and wears yellow rain slicker and hat. Butterfly, #1020, 3", 1979. $14-$18*

Snoopy. Sits and is dressed in red and white baseball outfit. Butterfly, #1022, 1979. $14-$18*

Snoopy. Sits and is dressed in a blue and white tennis outfit, carries a tennis racket, and wears a visor. Butterfly, #1021, 1979.

$8-$14*

Glass

Snoopy, sitting, Woodstock and the word "Friends" are etched inside. Heart-shaped. Butterfly, #1805, 3" x 2½", 1979. $30-$40*

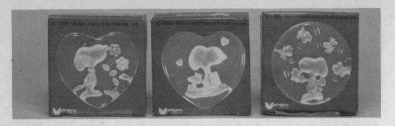

Snoopy, sniffing flowers, is etched inside. Heart-shaped. Butterfly, #1802, 3″ x 2½″, 1979. $30–$40*

Snoopy and Woodstock, sitting, and two small hearts are etched inside. Round. Butterfly, #1801, 3″ x 2½″, 1979. $30–$40*

Snoopy and Woodstock. Football theme. Round, dome-shaped with paper picture inside. Butterfly, #250 GP PW001, mid 1970s.
                                                                                    $15–$25*

Snoopy, with a tennis racket. Round, dome-shaped with paper picture inside. Butterfly, #250 GP PW003, mid 1970s. $15–$25*

Snoopy lying on his house. Clouds in the sky. Round, dome-shaped with paper picture inside. (Not pictured.) Butterfly, #250 GP PW002, mid 1970s. $15–$25*

Snoopy, holding flowers. Stippled glass. Determined, #8572, 4½″ x 3½″, late 1970s. $15–$25*

Woodstock. Stippled glass. Determined, #8576, 2½″ x 3″, late 1970s. $15–$20*

Silver

Snoopy, sitting. Leonard Silver, #9677, 3½″, 1980. $18–$25*

PEN AND PENCIL HOLDERS

Snoopy, sitting with blue ink bottle between his legs. Bottle has an opening on top to hold pen. Ceramic. Butterfly, 3½″, mid 1970s.
$20–$25*

Snoopy, standing next to blue ink bottle with open top. Ceramic. Butterfly, 4″, mid 1970s. $22–$27*

Snoopy, wearing red crash helmet. He sits on black tire that serves as pen holder. Ceramic. Butterfly, 3½″, mid 1970s. $20–$30*

Snoopy, wearing red crash helmet. He stands next to three black tires that are open at top. Ceramic. Butterfly, 4″, mid 1970s. $20–$30*

Snoopy, in a blue tennis visor. He sits next to open red tennis bag which is holding his tennis racket. Ceramic. Butterfly, 4″, mid 1970s. $20–$30*

Snoopy, in blue tennis visor. The handle of his racket is the pen holder. Ceramic. Butterfly, 4″, mid 1970s. $20–$25*

Snoopy statue with baseball hat and bat. Base is captioned: "World's Greatest Baseball Player." Comes with pen. Ceramic. Butterfly, 4", mid 1970s. $25-$30*

Snoopy, sitting on a red heart with holder for pen. Caption on base: "I Love You." Ceramic. Butterfly, 4", mid 1970s. $20-$25*

Snoopy, standing in front of large red heart that serves as pencil holder. Heart is captioned "I Love You." Ceramic. Butterfly, 3", mid 1970s. $20-$25*

Snoopy, hugging Woodstock. Both sit on a white base which has pen holder. Base is captioned "Love." Ceramic. Butterfly, 3", mid 1970s. $15-$20*

SNOWGLOBES

Snoopy, with scarf and ski cap. Snoopy is ice skating. Trees complete the scene. Simon Simple, PW 3/200, early 1970s. $25-$30*

Snoopy, lying on his house. Snow appears when the globe is shaken. Simon Simple, PW1/150, early 1970s. $20-$30*

Snoopy *is kissing* Lucy. Red Hearts float around when the globe is shaken. Butterfly, #4601, 1981. $15–$20*

Snoopy *and* Woodstock *as scouts.* Both are roasting marshmallows. Shake the globe and yellow stars appear. Butterfly, #4601, 1981.
                                                                 $15–$20*

WASTEBASKETS

Charlie Brown. Sits and looks at his report card. He receives an A + . He says, ''Good Grief!'' Reverse side: Snoopy graduates cum laude. Metal. Chein Co., 13″, early 1970s. $15–$25

Snoopy as *the* Flying Ace. Snoopy is standing and looking a bit conceited. Lucy, sitting, is holding a book and tells Snoopy, ''That World War I Act of Yours Drives Me Crazy!'' Reverse side: Snoopy, standing on his bullet-riddled house, shakes his fist. Thought balloon: ''Curse You Red Baron!'' Chein Co., 13″, early 1970s.
                                                                 $15–$25

Snoopy and Woodstock, dancing in front of Snoopy's house. Caption: "Snoopy." Reverse: Charlie Brown is bringing Snoopy his dinner. Metal. Chein Co., 16″, early 1970s. $15–$25

Snoopy, kissing Peppermint Patty. Snoopy is thinking, "Hi Sweetie." Reverse: Linus sucking his thumb is thinking, "I Wonder if Thumbs Ever Spoil?" Metal. Chein Co., 13″, early 1970s. $15–$25

Snoopy, as a director. Snoopy stands with Lucy and Charlie Brown. Thought balloon: "Ready on the Set." Reverse: Charlie Brown says, "I'm a Star." Metal. Chein Co., 13″, early 1970s. $15–$25

MIB (Mint In Box): Item in unopened box, box in excellent condition.

Mint Condition: Superior quality, box missing.

Good Condition: All parts are included. Item and/or box shows limited wear and tear.

Poor Condition: Major wear and tear. Parts may be missing.

Dolls and Clothes

Although dolls were among the first licensed *Peanuts* items, dating back to the Hungerford hard rubber dolls of 1958, most have not greatly appreciated in value.

Plush dolls, which have been around since 1968, are a case in point. Because so many of the plushes have been made through the years, many almost identical to the ones currently produced, the plushes cannot command high prices.

Going back to those original Hungerfords, we can see where availability and not age is the determining factor. Lucy, Charlie Brown, and Linus, even to this day, can be seen almost everywhere. On the other hand, Pigpen and Schroeder are much tougher to find and they fetch much higher prices. Schroeder, in particular, can be a find. What is little known about Schroeder in this group is that he comes with a separate white piano with a bust of Beethoven on top. The piano is almost impossible to find. Some collectors have been known to pay exhorbitant prices for the piano alone.

One other group of dolls that bucked the trend and found favor with *Peanuts* collectors is Ideal's Snoopy rag dolls—Snoopy as Astronaut, Snoopy as Magician, and Snoopy as Superstar. Mint in the box, each is worth in excess of $100.

CLOTHES

Dress Me Belle, Knickerbocker, #1581, 1983

Belle Miss Hollywood (pictured with rubber Dress Me Belle doll). The gown is pink with a sash reading "Miss Hollywood." Crown included in package. #1586. $10–$12*

Belle Western. This outfit contains a hat, skirt, jacket, and boots. #1588. $10–$12*

Belle Cape. This comes with a fur-trimmed cape and a muff. #1576. $10–$12*

Belle Tennis. The complete outfit consists of a pair of shoes, tennis dress, racket, and handbag. #1583. $10–$12*

Belle Old Fashioned Outfit. The dress has puffed sleeves and apron. Shoes and hat piece complete the outfit. #1574. $10–$12*

Belle Nightgown. This bedtime outfit includes a nightgown, slippers, and a mirror. #1585. $10–$12*

Belle Beach. This fun outfit includes a bathing suit, wrap-around skirt, beach shoes, and heart-shaped sunglasses. #1575. $10–$12*

Belle Jewels. This sparkling outfit consists of a dress, shoes, necklace, earrings, and a ring. #1577. $10–$12*

Belle Roller Disco. When discoing you must have a pair of tights, a dress, headband, handbag, and of course the skates. That is what Belle has. #1587. $10–$12*

Belle Ballet. This package contains a ballet dress with a tutu, headband, wand with a star on top, ballet slippers. #1584. $10–$12*

Belle Cheerleader. Belle's complete outfit consists of a dress, panties, jacket, shoes, and pompoms. #1578. $10–$12*

Belle Southern Belle. In this package you will find a dress, bonnet, and flower basket. #1579. $10–$12*

Dress Me Snoopy, Knickerbocker, #1580, 1983

Snoopy Beach Outfit. A complete outfit consists of bathing trunks, beach jacket, beach shoes, and sunglasses. #1596. $8–$10*

Snoopy Formal Outfit. This outfit is complete if it contains a tuxedo, shirt, cummerbund, shoes, and a bouquet of flowers. #1597.
$8–$10*

Snoopy Bathrobe. A complete package contains a bathrobe, slippers, and a scrub brush. #1595. $8–$10*

Snoopy Sport. To be a real tennis champ, you must have a tennis warm-up suit, tennis racket, and shoes. #1594.   *$8–$10**

Snoopy Rock Star. Be a rock star with a guitar, frilly satin top, and pants. #1599.   *$8–$10**

Snoopy Western. With a hat, shirt, boots, jacket, pants, and neckerchief you can be an authentic cowboy. All you need is the horse. #1598.   *$8–$10**

Lucy, Determined, #378 (pictured with plastic Lucy doll), early 1970s

Lucy Plays Baseball. A complete box consists of shoes, baseball cap, shirt, glove, bat, and ball. #671.   *$20–$25**

Lucy Nurse Set. In the package you will find a nurse's cap, jacket, shoes, stethoscope, and medicine bag. #672.   *$20–$25**

Lucy Goes Surfing. A complete outfit will include frog's feet, goggles, green and white surfboard, bathing suit, and towel in green and white polka dots. #673.   *$20–$25**

Lucy Plays Hockey. A hockey outfit should have a hockey stick, skates, puck, and a pink and yellow hat and scarf. #674.

$20–$25*

Charlie Brown, Determined, #377 (pictured with plastic Charlie Brown doll), early 1970s

Charlie Brown Plays Baseball. A complete package includes shoes, shirt, baseball cap, glove, bat, and ball. #661.   *$20–$25**

Charlie Brown Doctor Set. The box should contain white coat, medicine bag, shoes, head mirror, and a stethoscope. #662.   *$20–$25**

Charlie Brown Goes Surfing. If you have frog's feet, goggles, a surfboard in blue and white, and bathing trunks in blue and white, you have a complete outfit. #663.   *$20–$25**

Charlie Brown Plays Hockey. The box contains a green and yellow scarf and hat, hockey stick, puck, and skates. #654.   *$20–$25**

Snoopy, Determined, #376 (pictured with plastic Snoopy doll), early 1970s

Snoopy Plays Baseball. Snoopy is ready to go if he has shoes, shirt, baseball cap, bat, ball, and glove. #651.   *$20–$25**

Snoopy Doctor Set. This box contains a white coat, medicine bag, head mirror, shoes, and stethoscope. #652.   *$20–$25**

Snoopy Goes Surfing. To surf better you must have frog's feet and goggles, the surfboard, bathing trunks, and towel in colors of pink and yellow. #653. $20-$25*

Snoopy Plays Hockey. With skates, hockey stick, puck, and hat with scarf in green and yellow you are ready for your hockey game. #654. $20-$25*

DOLLS

Felt

Simon Simple, 7½", mid 1960s.

Charlie Brown, lightly stuffed and wearing red and black shirt.

$25-$35

Lucy, lightly stuffed and wearing a pink dress. $25-$35

Linus with his blanket, lightly stuffed. $25-$35

Paper

Snoopy with ten outfits. Description on package: ''Your favorite dog, Snoopy, has a whole new wardrobe . . . 10 separate outfits to cut out and stick on with the enclosed adhesive crayon.'' Determined, #274, 1976. $25-$30*

Plastic

Determined, #375, early 1970s.

Charlie Brown. He is wearing his baseball gear. Jointed. #377.
$20-$40*

Snoopy. Jointed. #376. $10-$25*

Lucy. She is wearing a red dress and saddle shoes. Jointed. #378.
$20-$40*

Plush

Snoopy, sitting. Felt eyes, eyebrows, and nose. Black spot on back. Red plastic tag around his neck has a picture of Snoopy. Captioned: "A *Peanuts* Character Plush Dog From the Peanuts Comic Strip." Determined, #833, 15″, 1971. $15-$30*

Snoopy, sitting. Felt eyes, eyebrows, and nose. Red paper tag around his neck. Tag has picture of Snoopy. Captioned: "A *Peanuts* Character Plush Dog From the *Peanuts* Comic Strip." Determined, #835, 12″, 1971. $10-$20*

Rag

Autograph Snoopy, sitting. Comes with pen. Determined, #838, 10½", 1971. $15-$25*

Playmate Snoopy, sitting. Solidly stuffed. Determined, #819, 6", 1971. $5-$20*

Ideal, 1976.

 Charlie Brown. His shirt is orange with a black zigzag design and his pants are black. Removable. #1412-6. $5-$30*

 Peppermint Patty. Her outfit of a green and white shirt with black pants is removable. #1413-4. $5-$30*

 Lucy. Her red dress with a blue collar and a blue stripe is removable. #1411-8. $5-$30*

 Linus. He is wearing a green and blue horizontal-striped shirt and black pants, both removable. #1414-2. $5-$30*

 Snoopy. Is the same as the rag doll Snoopy by Determined, but packed in a box the same as Charlie Brown, Linus, Lucy, and Peppermint Patty. $5-$50*

Snoopy, *wearing blue jeans and red shirt.* Shirt depicts members of
the gang. Shirt caption: "The Gang's All Here." (Same as the Snoopy
by Ideal, but Ideal's box is different.) Determined, 14″, late 1970s.
$5-$50*

Snoopy *as Astronaut.* He wears a helmet and an astronaut suit. Ideal,
#1441-5, 14″, 1977. $50-$140*

Snoopy *as Magician.* He wears a cape, high hat, formal wear, and
sports a long mustache. Ideal, #1448-0, 14″, 1977. $50-$125*

Snoopy *as Rock Star.* He wears a wig, outrageous Elton John-type
shoes, and holds a plastic microphone. Ideal, #1446-4, 14″, 1977.
$40-$130*

Rubber

Astronaut, Snoopy. Rubber head, plastic body, plastic bubble, life support system. Space suit is regulation NASA fabric. Snoopy is wearing his traditional Flying Ace scarf. Determined, #808, 1969.

$15–$25*

COLLECTOR DOLLS, DETERMINED, 8″, 1982

Belle, wears a red jacket and blue pants and sports her walkman.

$25–$35

Snoopy, has on earphones and sports his walkman over his shoulder. He is wearing a red jacket and blue pants.

$20–$30

Snoopy, The Soccer Player. Snoopy is wearing a red and white shirt, red pants, and the soccer ball is held in a net bag. #3404.

$25–$35*

Snoopy, wearing a tuxedo.

$20–$30

Snoopy, The Tennis Player. Snoopy has on a tennis outfit, and a tennis bag with a racket in it. #3403.

$25–$35*

Snoopy, The Baseball Player. Snoopy is outfitted in a typical baseball outfit with a baseball cap and glove. #3405.

$25–$35*

Snoopy, The Golfer. Snoopy wears a yellow, green, and white outfit, cap, and carries a golf bag with clubs.

$30–$40*

Snoopy, The Sailor. A complete outfit includes a white terrycloth hooded jacket, red and white shirt, blue pants, and shoes. #3406.

$25–$35*

Snoopy, The Roller Skater. Snoopy is wearing a red, white, and blue outfit and skates. #3401.

$30–$40*

Snoopy, The Jogger. Snoopy is outfitted in a brown sweatsuit and headband. #3402.

$25–$35*

Belle as The Bride. A headpiece and bridal gown are worn by Belle.

$25–$35

Belle in Dolly Madison style red and white outfit.

$25–$35

"DRESS ME" DOLLS, KNICKERBOCKER, 1983

Dress Me Belle. Belle is wearing a pink dress with blue dots and a blue ribbon in her hair. #1581. (See section on "Clothes" for outfit shown.)

$12–$35*

Dress Me Snoopy. Snoopy is wearing blue jeans and a red and yellow shirt captioned "Snoopy." #1580. (See section on "Clothes" for outfit shown.)

$15–$30*

HUNGERFORD DOLLS, HUNGERFORD PLASTICS CORP., 1958

The following are commonly known as Hungerford dolls. Mint in the package with the cartoon panel on top is extremely rare. Their clothes are painted on.

Charlie Brown. He is in a red shirt with zigzag black design and black pants, 8½". $20–$75*

Lucy. She has on a yellow dress and a yellow beanie, 8½".

$20–$75*

Pigpen. He is wearing blue overalls, 8½". $60–$100*

Snoopy, sitting, 7". $35–$75*

Linus with his blanket, 8½". $25–$75*

Sally, sitting. She is in a red sleeper with a flap in the back, 6½".

$50–$85*

Schroeder and his piano (which is not attached to Schroeder). He is wearing red pajamas, 7". $150–$200*

Charlie Brown, 7³/₄". $40–$110*

Lucy, 7¹/₄". $45–$130*

Linus with blanket, 7". $45–$130*

Snoopy, 5¹/₂". $50 –$130*

PLAYABLES (FLAT. CLOTHES PAINTED ON.), DETERMINED, 1969

Snoopy, #843, 4¹/₄". $5–$25*

Charlie Brown. Chuck is wearing an orange baseball hat, baseball glove (painted on), red shirt with zigzag design, and black pants. #840, 5¹/₄". $5–$25*

Lucy. She is wearing a pink dress. #842, 5". $5–$25*

Linus with red blanket. He is wearing a red and white shirt and black pants. #841, 5". $10–$25*

An asterisk (*) next to a price indicates that the item comes with its original box in excellent condition. If no asterisk is shown, there is no box or the box adds little significant value. Shipping boxes (no graphics) are of no value.

———————————

A copyright date indicates the year the character first appeared in a particular incarnation, *not* the year the product first came out.

POCKET DOLLS, BOUCHER AND CO., 7″, 1968

Linus. He is wearing a red and white shirt and black pants. And, of course, his red blanket. #801. $5–$9*

Lucy. She is wearing a pink dress. Her mouth is wide open—more like the fussbudget Lucy that we know. #802. $8–$13*

Charlie Brown. He is wearing a red shirt with a black zigzag design, black pants, and a rust and black baseball cap. #800. $4–$8*

Schroeder. He is wearing black pants and an orange shirt with Beethoven's face and name on it. #804. $7–$12*

Lucy. She is wearing a pink dress. She has a smile on her face. #802. $5–$10*

Snoopy. He is wearing his Flying Ace outfit which includes brown helmet and blue scarf. #803. $3–$8*

Stuffed

Pillow Dolls. Stuffed with kapok. The clothes are part of the fabric's design. Determined, late 1960s.

    Lucy, #812, 17½″. $5–$20*

    Schroeder, with Beethoven's picture on the front of his blue shirt, #814, 17½″. $15–$20*

    Linus, #811, 15½″. $10–$20*

    Charlie Brown, #810, 16″. $5–$20*

    Snoopy, #813, 14″. $5–$20*

Figurals

Figural is the term for a full-figured or three-dimensional character. This is an excellent category for beginning collectors. Most figurals, particularly the trophies, are easy to find and consequently are not expensive. You will be encouraged by the progress you make in a very short time. But, please do not go overboard on the price.

You will find the articulated ceramic Snoopy a beautiful item to own. "Articulated" means that the arms and legs are movable at the joints.

Bobbleheads and nodders—the words are interchangeable, but Lego preferred to use "nodders"—are those desirable pieces whose heads are on a spring, giving them a nodding effect at the slightest vibration.

The Lego nodder is a delicate older piece that is susceptible to cracks and is therefore very hard to come by in mint condition. Until you find the superior piece, you may have to settle for one that has minor chinks or blemishes (at less than mint price, of course).

Plastic trophies were first introduced in 1970 with the 5″ "World's Greatest" Snoopy as the Flying Ace. Four other distinct styles of trophies eventually found their way to the market: the "sparkies" in 1971 followed by the 3″ trophy, the mini trophy pin, and the large scenic trophies.

It was the combination of the *Peanuts* characters, the thought or title they expressed (for example: "World's Greatest Father"), and their comparatively low prices that made the 5″ trophy extremely popular with the public. Over 100 different pieces were produced. Once purchased, however, the 5″ trophy did not have staying power. Many soon wound up in garage sales and flea markets.

You will notice that many of the 5″ trophies in this chapter are in the $5–$8 range. The reader, however, should not infer that all 5″ trophies are worth that much. We deliberately included only trophies where the characters were presented in an unusual way or trophies that are less plentiful. Unless there is something special to recommend them, you will find trophies at flea markets for $1–$2 and sometimes as little as 50 cents.

Many stores originally removed the trophy from the box. Not to worry. The boxes were primarily designed for mailing. This is one of those items whose value is not materially increased by the presence of a box.

Because Aviva was successful in producing such large quantities of so many different 5″ trophies—and kept most of them continually in production for well over a decade from 1969 to the mid 1980s with no changes—and because many of the records of Aviva, which is no longer in business, are unavailable, it is almost impossible to track down the exact dates that most of the 5″ trophies first came out. For this reason, we omitted dates from the description of the 5″ trophies. In fact, because they were produced over such a long period of time, it might even be misleading if the dates were identified. After all, a trophy that first came out in 1972 might just as easily have been made in 1976 or 1983, and no collector would be any the wiser.

The larger scenic trophy is a little rarer than the 5″ and comes in a more attractive box. The mini trophy pin, 2½″ in height, includes both the base and a pin which can be removed and worn.

Sparkies have all the characteristics of trophies except one. They have no written message or thought. Since they are not seen frequently, they are at the top of the category valuewise.

FIGURES, CERAMIC

Articulated Snoopy. His arms and legs move. Determined, 12″ (sitting), early 1980s. $100–$200

Snoopy. He's shown in four different positions: sitting, leaning on his back, attempting to stand on his head, and standing on his head. Determined, tallest Snoopy is approximately 2½″, early 1980s.

Each $12–$15

FIGURESCENES, PAPIER-MÂCHÉ

"America You're Beautiful." Snoopy as Uncle Sam holding his hand on his heart. Determined, #776, 6½″, early 1970s. $25–$30*

"It's Hero Time." Snoopy wearing a ribbon medal. Determined, #771, 5½″, early 1970s. $15–$25*

"*Even My Anxieties Have Anxieties.*" Lucy and Charlie Brown at Lucy's psychiatrist booth. Determined, #769, 5″, early 1970s.

$45–$55*

"*How Can We Lose When We're So Sincere.*" Linus, Schroeder, Charlie Brown, Snoopy, and Lucy in baseball gear sitting or standing on one base together. Determined, #790, 4½″, early 1970s.

$90–$125*

"*I Look Forward to the Day When I'll Understand Men.*" Lucy leaning on Schroeder's piano while he plays. Determined, #762, 4½″, early 1970s.

$45–$55*

"*I've Developed a New Philosophy—I Dread One Day at a Time.*" Linus and Charlie Brown sitting on a bench. Determined, #766, 5″, early 1970s.

$35–$40*

"*I Made 120 Decisions Today . . . All of Them Wrong.*" Charlie Brown wearing a baseball cap. Determined, #778, 5¼", early 1970s.
$25–$30*

"*To Know Me Is to Love Me.*" Linus wearing a baseball cap and holding his blanket. Determined, #777, 5", early 1970s. $20–$25*

"*Look Out—I'm Going to Be Crabby All Day!*" Lucy standing. Determined, #772, 5¼", early 1970s. $20–$25*

"*I'm Allergic to Morning.*" Bleary-eyed Snoopy is lying on his tummy, on the roof of his house. Determined, #763, 4½", early 1970s. $10–$15*

"*Bleah!*" Lucy stands and sticks out her tongue. Determined, #768, 5¼", early 1970s. $15–$20*

"*Joe Cool.*" Snoopy wears an orange turtleneck sweater as well as shades. Determined, 5¼", early 1970s. $20–$25*

"*Love Is Walking Hand in Hand.*" Linus and Sally holding hands. Determined, #761, 5", early 1970s. $12–$20*

"*Happiness Is Having Someone to Lean On.*" Charlie Brown and Snoopy leaning close to one another. Determined, #760, 5", early 1970s. $8–$12*

"*I'm Thinking of You.*" Linus is sitting under a tree. Determined, #770, 5½", early 1970s. $20–$25*

"*My Secretary Isn't Worth Anything Before Coffee Break.*" Snoopy and Woodstock at the typewriter. Determined, #767, 4½", early 1970s. $25–$35*

"*He's a Nice Guy But I Don't Know Where He Stands.*" Snoopy, sitting. Woodstock holding a sign with a paper question mark on it. Determined, #775, 4½", early 1970s. $35–$45*

"*Perhaps Some Dark Haired Lass Will Share My Table.*" Snoopy as the Flying Ace is seated behind an oval table covered with a red and white tablecloth. A bottle of root beer is there, all ready for Snoopy to quaff. Determined, #773, 5", early 1970s. $25–$35*

NODDERS AND BOBBLEHEADS, PAPIER-MÂCHÉ

Bobbleheads

This was the name given by the manufacturer to its nodders. The head is on a spring and can, therefore, bounce and "nod" when moved.

Determined, 4″, 1976.

    Snoopy as Santa. $15–$20

    Snoopy, sitting. $10–$15

    Snoopy wearing an orange sweater with ''Joe Cool'' written on it. $10–$20

    Snoopy as the Flying Ace. $10–$20

    Woodstock, holding a pink flower. $15–$20

    Lucy, wearing a red dress. $15–$25

    Charlie Brown wearing baseball cap. $15–$25

Nodders

The phrase ''of the *Peanuts* comic strip'' appears below each name. The head is on a spring and, therefore, can bounce and ''nod'' when moved.

Lego, 5½″, 1959.

    Pigpen (spelled Pig Pen on nodder; Pigpen is correct). $35–$60

    Linus. $35–$60

    Schroeder. His white shirt shows a decal: a bust of Beethoven on a piano. $35–$65

Charlie Brown.	$35–$60
Snoopy.	$35–$60
Lucy.	$35–$60

TROPHIES

2″ Message Trophies, Aviva, 1974

Snoopy wearing disco jacket situated on a pedestal. Caption: "Saturday Night Beagle." Ceramic. $2–$3

Snoopy lying on top of house situated on a pedestal. Caption: "Get Well." Ceramic. $2–$3

Snoopy wearing party hat and holding a gift situated on a pedestal. Caption: "Congratulations." Ceramic. $2–$3

3″ Mini-Grams, Aviva, 1972

Snoopy at the typewriter. Caption: "Hello." Plastic. $5–$8*

Snoopy dancing. Caption: "Snoopy." Plastic. $5–$8*

Snoopy with outstretched hand. Caption: "Congratulations." Plastic. $5–$8*

Snoopy holding empty supper dish. Caption: "Thank you." Plastic. $5–$8*

5″ Trophies, Aviva

Snoopy as the Flying Ace. Caption: "World's Greatest." (First design made originally in 1969 and repeated through mid 1980s.) Plastic. $1.50–$3

Linus and his blanket. Caption: "We All Have Our Hangups." Plastic. $5–$8

Snoopy holding Uncle Sam hat. Caption: "America You're Beautiful." Plastic. $5–$8

Lucy and Charlie Brown at psychiatrist booth. Caption: "Keep the Corners of Your Mouth Turned Up." Plastic. $5–$8

Snoopy dressed as George Washington with hatchet. Caption: "Spirit of '76 1776–1976." Plastic.. $5–$8

Snoopy wearing big red wig while doing Woodstock's hair. Caption: "World's Greatest Hair Stylist." Plastic. $1.50–$3

Snoopy grinning as he walks. Caption: "This is a Difficult Time . . . I'm Going Through Life." Plastic. $1.50–$3

Snoopy resting under tree while Woodstock works. Caption: "Working Is for the Birds." Plastic. $1.50–$3

Peppermint Patty. Caption: "You Are a Rare Gem." Plastic.
$5–$8

Snoopy holds sign with paw print. Caption: "Paw Power." Plastic.
$8–$10

Scenic Trophies, Aviva, Early 1970s

Snoopy looking in the mirror. Caption: "You're the Fairest One of All." Plastic, 4½" x 3¾". $8-$12*

Snoopy with bow and arrow, heart, and Woodstock. Caption: "You've Captured My Heart." Plastic, 4½" x 3¾". $10-$15*

Sparkies (mounted on teakwood base), Aviva, 1971–1972

Snoopy throwing frisbee that is on a spring. Woodstock in front right corner. Plastic, 5½". $20-$25*

Snoopy as the Flying Ace on his house that is on a spring. Woodstock in front right corner. Plastic, 7". $20-$25*

Snoopy, dancing, on spring. Woodstock in front right corner. Plastic, 5½". $20-$25*

Snoopy on spring, flying kite. Woodstock in front left corner. Plastic, 8½". $20-$25*

Trophy Pins, Aviva, Early 1970s

Snoopy on dog house. Woodstock inside. Caption on stand: "Howdy." Plastic, 2½". $6–$8*

Snoopy as Flying Ace. Caption: "I Care Not For Fame & Glory." Plastic, 2½". $6–$8*

Snoopy and Woodstock in his dish. Caption: "Smile." Caption on stand: "You Don't Know What You're Missing." Plastic, 2½".
                                                $6–$8*

MIB (Mint In Box): Item in unopened box, box in excellent condition.

Mint Condition: Superior quality, box missing.

Good Condition: All parts are included. Item and/or box shows limited wear and tear.

Poor Condition: Major wear and tear. Parts may be missing.

Hallmark, Ambassador, and Springbok— Paper and Related Items

While 1990 marks the fortieth anniversary of *Peanuts*, it is significant to note that this year is also the thirtieth anniversary of Hallmark's association with the gang as one of the earliest and most important licensees.

This "partnership" has helped influence an important part of Americana in the latter half of the twentieth century. To the serious collector, the Hallmark affiliation was a milestone in the history of *Peanuts*.

Hallmark's *Peanuts* greeting cards, one Get Well card, one Baby card, and two Birthday cards, first hit the stores in 1960. These were an immediate success and were quickly followed by bridge tallies, party goods, and mini-posters. It was through Hallmark stores that many Americans were first introduced to *Peanuts*.

With its large number of retail outlets nationwide, Hallmark contributed immensely toward the mushrooming popularity of *Peanuts*. Not only did the Hallmark gift stores carry the complete line of *Peanuts* Hallmark products, they also sold enormous quantities of merchandise from Determined, Aviva, Butterfly, and other licensees. So important was the Hallmark connection, that as late as the mid 1970s many collectors thought that Hallmark stores were the only places you could find *Peanuts* items. And indeed, since department stores did not fully catch up to the *Peanuts* boom until the late 1970s, they almost were.

You will note several items with Ambassador and Springbok labels in this chapter. The reason is that both companies are divisions of Hallmark.

CARDBOARD STANDUPS

Charlie Brown, with a paper ornament attached to his hand. Caption: "Merry Christmas." Inside caption: "And Other Salutations of the Season." Comes with a heavy cardboard mailer. Hallmark, #250X202–3, 24″ x 17″, 1967.

$30–$40

Lucy, holding a message between her two hands. Caption: "Merry Christmas to Someone I'm Immensely Fond Of." Comes with a heavy cardboard mailer. Hallmark, #250X203–6, 24″ x 16″, 1967.

$30–$40

Pigpen. He says, "If You're Going to Be an Ecologist You've Got to Stir Things Up a Little." Hallmark, 9½″, early 1970s. $5–$8

Snoopy. Thought balloon: "Nobody Ever Calls Me 'Sugarlips'." Hallmark, #50KF 851–6, 9½", early 1970s. $5–$8

Snoopy. Wearing a visor and holding a tennis racket. Hallmark, #200HD 99–1, 21", 1972. $20–$25

NOVELTIES

Flip books on a metal ring. Comic strips presented in flip top sequence. Hallmark, 3" x 3", early 1970s.

Live & Learn. Cover: Linus seated at a desk. #100RB2–6. $7–$12

Charlie Brown's World. Cover: round face and hands of Charlie Brown. #100RB2–8. $7–$12

Love, Sweet Love. Cover: Charlie Brown being hugged by Snoopy. #100RB2–1. $7–$12

Hand-held fans. Springbok, 8¾" x 9¼", 1974.

Snoopy on surfboard rides a wave. "Cowabunga!" Reverse side: Snoopy holding a surfboard. "Surf's Up!" #100S1P202–3.

$10–$15

Sally with her hair sticking out says, "Thought for the Summer . . ." Reverse side: "Never Play Jacks on a Hot Sidewalk!" 100S1P202–4. $10–$15

Snoopy Gourmet Guide. A flip pad of 12 recipes, each accompanied by a different Snoopy cartoon. Cover: Snoopy in chef's hat and bib sits with knife and fork in front of his house. Hallmark, #200M400–5, 14″, 1967. $18–$25

PARTY AND GIFT ACCESSORIES

Cake decoration. Snoopy as the Flying Ace is in the center. Snoopy, ten candle holders, six Woodstocks, and "Happy Birthday" are all edible. Hallmark, #100PF97–2, mid 1970s. $8–$15*

Centerpiece. Snoopy is lying on his doghouse holding a "Happy Birthday" pennant. Hallmark, late 1960s. $15–$20*

Centerpiece. "Linus and the Great Pumpkin." Linus is leaning on the pumpkin. Snoopy is inside a paper pumpkin holding a sign captioned "Welcome Great Pumpkin." Hallmark, #150HYP144, early 1970s. $15–$25*

Cups, paper. Linus and Lucy watch Snoopy dancing with kite. Hallmark, 9 oz., #49DC97–1, early 1970s. $3–$5*

Decoration pressout book. Cover: Snoopy, Linus, and Woodstock are in the pumpkin patch. Caption: "Great Pumpkin." Hallmark, #100HHD 4–9, early 1970s. $15–$20

Decoration pressout book. Cover: Snoopy's face is inside a Christmas wreath. Characters are superimposed on actual photographs. Caption: "Merry Christmas." Hallmark, #100XHD 28–4, mid 1970s.
                                                      $15–$20

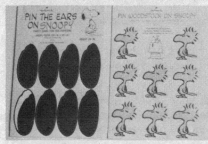

Game, Pin the Ears on Snoopy. Eight black pressout ears and 20 colored pins are used to pin a dancing Snoopy. Hallmark, #150HD 97–7, 20″ x 20½″, early 1970s. $10–$18*

Game, Pin Woodstock on Snoopy. Snoopy lies on his back atop his house, with Woodstock on his tummy. Seven pressout Woodstocks and a pack of colored pins are included. Hallmark, #150HD 100–3, 20″ x 20½″, early 1970s. $10–$18*

Gift wrap. A busy collage of the *Peanuts* gang at a party, including Snoopy in a fancy jacket dancing with Peppermint Patty. Hallmark, #50EW 1524, early 1970s. $2–$4*

Gift wrap, Christmas. Scenes depict Schroeder at the piano with a Beethoven bust wearing a red Santa hat on the piano; Charlie Brown's kite caught on Christmas tree; Snoopy lying on his house and dreaming of a pizza; Lucy and Linus are making a snowman; and Lucy is singing while Linus and Charlie Brown cover their ears. Ambassador, #35 XW300, late 1960s. $4–$6*

Gift wrap 'n trim, Christmas. Lucy at her booth captioned "Christmas Advice 5¢ Holiday Rates." Charlie Brown is holding a gift box, Linus is making a snowman, Snoopy as the Flying Ace is pulling a sleigh. Woodstock is wearing a stocking cap. The gift tag is a large Charlie Brown. Hallmark, #75XE 4055, early 1970s. $4–$6*

Glasses, plastic. Snoopy as the Flying Ace in four different designs. Caption: "Snoopy and the Red Baron." Hallmark, #125 DC 60K, 10 oz., early 1970s. $8–$12*

Glasses, plastic. Snoopy, Linus, Lucy, and Charlie Brown each saying or thinking something are featured on the "*Peanuts* Pak of Party Glasses." Hallmark, #125 DC 60K, 10 oz., early 1970s. $8–$12*

Invitation, Halloween. Linus is in the pumpkin patch. Snoopy is coming up out of a pumpkin holding a sign captioned "Join Us at the Pumpkin Patch." Hallmark, #60HIN14–4, early 1970s. $4–$6*

Invitation, A Barbecue. Snoopy wears a chef's apron and uses a bone to bang on his supper dish. Hallmark, #75PM 12–9, early 1970s. $3–$5*

Napkins, beverage. "Snoopy For President." Box of 32 with four designs. Cover of box: Snoopy as the Flying Ace. Caption: "A Distinguished Combat Hero!!" The other three designs featuring Lucy, Linus, and Charlie Brown are shown on the back of the box. Hallmark, #100NK97–2, 5″ x 5″, early 1970s. $5–$10*

Napkins, beverage. "Snoopy and the Red Baron." Box of 32. Cover of box: Snoopy on bullet-riddled house thinking "Rats!" The four different designs are shown on back of box. Hallmark, #100NK97–5, 5″ x 5″, early 1970s. $12–$15*

Napkins, luncheon. Snoopy on his house eating, with Woodstock sitting next to him. Lucy holds a sandwich in her hand and says to Snoopy, "You Call This Peanut Butter Sandwich a Party?" Hallmark, #65NKZ97–4, 13½″ × 13½″, mid 1970s. $3–$4*

Plates, paper. Snoopy with supper dish on his head, Woodstock in dish. Sally, Schroeder, Lucy, Charlie Brown complete the cast. Circular caption: "Hail! Hail! The Gang's All Here!" Hallmark, #50DP 97–4, 7″, mid 1970s. $3–$4*

Plates, paper. Snoopy as the Flying Ace jumping on his house that has a bull's-eye on it. Woodstock falls off onto his head. Caption: "KA-BAM! WHUMP! KA-CHUNK! RIP! CLUNK!" Hallmark, #65DP97–2, 9″, mid 1970s. $3–$4*

Spoons and forks. Snoopy is on the top of each of the four plastic forks and the four spoons. Caption: "Snoopy Super Service: . . ." Hallmark, #100PW96–7, early 1970s. $8–$12*

Toothpicks. Snoopy is on top of each of the 12 plastic picks. Hallmark, #100PF 101–8, early 1970s (see photo on previous page, bottom right). $6–$10*

Tablecloth, paper. Among the scenes: Schroeder is at his piano, Peppermint Patty says to Snoopy, ''Let's Sit the Next One Out, Crazylegs.'' Hallmark, #125TF 97–4, 60″ x 102″ (also came in 44″ x 44″), mid 1970s. $4–$6*

Tablecloth, paper. Snoopy reads a Valentine's Day card while sitting on Charlie Brown's tummy. Above him is a mailbox. Hallmark, #100VTA 2–5, 60″ x 102″, mid 1970s. $8–$10*

PLAYING CARDS

Double deck. Snoopy on his tummy lies on a large pink-orange balloon. Other deck shows Snoopy dancing, same colored background. Hallmark, mid 1970s. $18–$30*

Double deck. Deck one has Snoopy smiling on his house as the Flying Ace. Red circles in the background. Deck two has Snoopy as the Flying Ace, standing and angry. Blue circles in the background. Hallmark, mid 1970s. $18–$30*

Ensemble. Deck one shows Woodstock sitting on Snoopy's head holding flowers. Blue background. Deck two has Woodstock leaning against Snoopy who now has the flowers. Red background. The score pad cover repeats the design of deck one, except for red background. A mechanical pencil is included. Hallmark, 1976. $25–$35*

Game Cards. Hallmark, 1975.

Security. Linus sitting with his blanket. #125BC98–1. $15–$20*

Rats. Snoopy as the Flying Ace sits on a bullet-riddled house. #125BC99–3. $10–$15*

Fussbudget. Lucy with her widemouth look. #125BC98–2.
     $15–$20*

Mini. 2½″ x 1¾″. Mint box has a seal, usually gold, with Snoopy lying on his house. Hallmark (except Charlie Brown), early 1970s.

Snoopy with jelly beans, #100BC118–7. $9–$15*

Linus with his blanket, #75BC98–9. $9–$15*

Charlie Brown (Ambassador), #88BC78OJ. $9–$15*

Lucy as a cheerleader, #100BC121–2. $8–$12*

Snoopy lying on his house with a big bubble on his nose. The entire background is colored bubbles, #100BC118–8. $8–$10*

Snoopy as Joe Cool, #75BC101–9. $6–$10*

Single decks. Hallmark, 3½″ x 2¼″, 1974.

Charlie Brown hugging Snoopy. Pink background with red hearts. #125BC99–7. $12–$18*

Snoopy in a raccoon coat and carrying "Rah" pennant. #125BC99–6.
     $10–$15*

POSTERS

Pigpen. Pigpen says, "If You're Going to Be an Ecologist, You've Got to Stir Things Up a Little." Dirt and dust all around him. Springbok, #PTR 302–3, 1971. $12–$20

Snoopy. Thought balloon: "Support the Olympics . . . Hug an Athlete." Springbok, #200PTR3025, 1971. $12–$20

Snoopy in the ocean on a surfboard. Thought balloon: "Cowabunga." Springbok, 1972. $12–$20

Snoopy and Woodstocks. Thought balloon: "Life is One Big Thrill After Another." Springbok, 1972. $14–$22

SCRAPBOOKS AND PHOTOGRAPH ALBUMS

Album, looseleaf type. Caption: "The *Peanuts* Thoughtfulness Album." Snoopy is lying on a mailbox. There is an older looking Woodstock with a letter. Inside there are pictures of the gang, folders, and a calendar. Hallmark, 10″ x 8″, early 1970s. $25–$35

Album, photograph. Caption: "Snaps, Scraps and Souvenirs." Cover design: Linus looks at Lucy who is on her tummy looking at her book. Inside, each page has red, white, and black pictures of the gang. Hallmark, #400SB 10–1, 11¼″ x 9″, early 1970s. $20–$30

Album, photograph. Cover design: Linus with a camera around his neck. Caption: "Want to See My Pictures?" Inside are several pictures of the gang in red, white, and black. Hallmark, #250PHA 105–1, early 1970s. $15–$20

Album, photograph. Charlie Brown sits at a school desk with raised hand. Caption: "Don't You Just Love School?" Hallmark, #250PHA 106–1, 1972. $15–$20

Album, photograph. Cover design: Snoopy carrying hobo pack. Caption: "It Was a Great Trip." Hallmark, #250PHA 108–1, 1972 (see photo on previous page, bottom right). $10–$20

Scrapbook. Cover design: Snoopy with a book shares the roof of his house with Woodstock. Cover is green, white, and blue. Caption: "Scraps." Hallmark, #450 PA 60 5–5, 10¾″ x 9″, early 1970s.

$15–$25

STATIONERY AND GREETING CARDS

Cards, Christmas. Twenty-five boxed. In colors of red, white, and black. Designs with Lucy, Snoopy, Linus or Charlie Brown in a Christmas-related activity. Hallmark, #200BX69–1, late 1960s.

$10–$15*

Cards, Valentine's Day. Cylindrical box in colors of red, pink, white, and black. Box front shows Snoopy hugging Charlie Brown while Lucy looks on. Hallmark, #125 BV2–9, late 1960s. $20–$25*

An asterisk (*) next to a price indicates that the item comes with its original box in excellent condition. If no asterisk is shown, there is no box or the box adds little significant value. Shipping boxes (no graphics) are of no value.

A copyright date indicates the year the character first appeared in a particular incarnation, *not* the year the product first came out.

Peanuts Pen 'N Note Ensemble. Stationery design is done in red, white, and black. Pen and paper notes have Linus, Lucy, Charlie Brown, and Snoopy. The flap of the envelope has Snoopy's head peering out of the mailbox. Hallmark; #200 EM 382–1, late 1960s.

$10–$15*

Pop Up Cards (Original Price 50¢)

Birthday. Cover: Schroeder, carrying piano, walks with four-legged Snoopy. Caption: "Thought I'd Wish You a Happy Birthday . . ." Inside pop up: Schroeder at the piano; Snoopy is sitting on it; Frieda is singing; Lucy conducting; Linus, Violet, Charlie Brown, Sally are playing instruments. Hallmark, #50B 400–7, mid 1960s. $4–$6

Get Well. Cover: Charlie Brown is in baseball gear saying, "Sure Sorry You're Sick. . . ." Inside pop up: Lucy, Sally, Schroeder, Charlie Brown, Linus, Frieda, Snoopy are all sitting on a bench. Caption: "Hope You're Back in the Line-Up Soon!" Hallmark, #50 C 400–6, mid 1960s. $7–$10

Vacation. Cover: Snoopy running with a surfboard. Thought balloon: "Going on Vacation?" Inside pop up: Snoopy surfing on waves. Caption: "Have a Great Trip!" Hallmark, #50 M 600–1, mid 1960s. $7–$10

Household Furnishings and Everyday Items

When the anthropologists come to investigate the remnants of our society a millennium from now, they will almost certainly come to the conclusion that in our homes, at least, we had a particular fascination for a beagle that walks on its hind legs, five or six yellow birds, a round-faced kid named Charlie Brown, and a whole bunch of his playmates whose favorite game was baseball. (We leave it to the anthropologists to determine if the team ever scored a run.)

Although the items in this chapter are more mundane in nature, they are reflective of the pervasive influence of *Peanuts* in our homes and our lives. It seems that at one time or another half the homes in America had at least one room—usually the pre-adolescent's—designed with a *Peanuts* or Snoopy theme. *Peanuts* products served a utilitarian function in many other parts of the home as well.

Simon Simple was one of the early leaders in this area. In the mid 1960s it came out with pajama bags that were highlighted with felt. To this day, if you see something accented with felt, the chances are it is a Simon Simple item.

One noteworthy item in this chapter is the 1962 calendar by Determined Productions. With this calendar was launched the company that soon grew to be the world's biggest *Peanuts* licensee. Determined practically owned the fields of ornaments, calendars, ceramic planters, mugs, figural statues, banks, banners, and plush dolls. In addition to introducing the plushes Snoopy, Belle, Spike, and Woodstock, Determined created stylish wardrobes for them as well. Exhibits of Snoopy and Belle modelling elegant designer clothes have toured throughout the world and are frequently displayed even today. The innovations and creative influence of Determined and its dynamic president Connie Boucher went beyond *Peanuts* to impact the product/marketing world.

Calendars, incidentally, are an excellent example of collectors buying two pieces, one to use and one to save.

In the ceramic/glass section, take particular note of the "Snoopy lying on his house" cookie jar. It is a rarity and a favorite with collectors.

Another favorite of ours is the *Peanuts* napkins that Monogram came out with in the early 1960s. The box cover and the comic strips on the napkins themselves reflect the look of the characters in their earlier years. This collectible shows Violet, an important character in the earliest comic strips. However, she never achieved the prominence of some of the other characters and soon faded into the background.

ASSORTED ITEMS

Bubble Bucket (name used by manufacturer). The knob of the lift-off cover is Snoopy's head. His body is immersed in pastel-colored bubbles. Caption on the front of the bucket: "Bubble Bath." Ceramic. Determined, #8453, 5½" x 3½", 1979. $20–$30

Bubble Tub (name used by manufacturer). The knob of the lift-off cover is Snoopy's head. His body is immersed in pastel-colored bubbles, and one bubble is on his nose. Determined, #8458, 4½" x 3", 1979. $20–$30

Cake plate on a pedestal. Snoopy is pictured as a chef holding a cake. Woodstocks and Snoopy are shown in front of a dessert display. Melmac. Brookpark, 12" diam., 1979. $30–$40*

Candy dish, ceramic. Snoopy is shown wearing a ribbon that is captioned "Great." Woodstock is giving him a flower. Caption: "I'm Not Perfect But I'm Pretty Perfect." Determined, #8824, 2″ x 4½″, 1976. $12–$18

Canister set. Triple-nested. Wraparound cartoon art. Metal. Large canister: Snoopy is sitting at a table in a cafe (side in view), 6¼″ x 7¾″ d. Medium canister: Snoopy as a chef holds a frying pan and Woodstock is sitting in it (side in view), 5″ x 6¾″ d. Small canister: Snoopy looks out from underneath a tablecloth (picture in view), 4⅜″ x 5¾″ d. Determined, #0367, 1979.   Set $30–$45

Christmas box, ceramic. A raised Snoopy as Santa Claus decorates the lift-off lid. Determined, 4½″ x 2¾″ x 2″, late 1970s. $20–$25

Christmas box, ceramic. A raised Woodstock and Snoopy are dressed in Santa outfits and surrounded by some gift packages on the lift-off lid. The raised lettering reads: "Merry Christmas." Determined, 4½″ x 2¾″ x 2″, late 1970s. $25–$35

Cookie jar, ceramic. Commonly called the chef cookie jar because Snoopy's chef's hat becomes the lift-off lid. The yellow neckerchief completes his outfit. Determined, #0983, 7½″, 1979. $15–$25

Cookie jar, ceramic. Commonly known as the large chef cookie jar. Snoopy wears a yellow neckerchief and his chef's hat is the lift-off lid. Determined, #8480, 11", 1977. $50–$60

Cookie jar in the shape of Snoopy's doghouse. Has a red lift-off roof and white base. Snoopy is lying on top. Determined/McCoy, 11", early 1970s. $80–$125

Cutting board. Non-cutting side shows Snoopy and Woodstock in chefs' hats. Snoopy is preparing a special Snoopy salad in his bowl while Woodstock is perched on the pepper grinder. Brookpark, 8" x 10" plus 5" handle, 1979. $20–$30

Dog bone jar, ceramic. Knob of the lift-off cover is Snoopy's head and shoulders. Caption on jar: "Snoopy Brown Bag Pet Goodies." Con Agra, #71–63428–7, 6" x 5" x 13", early 1980s. $60–$80*

Egg cup, *ceramic*. A full-figure Snoopy, wearing a yellow necker-chief, has a depression in the top of his chef's hat. A perfect place to put that egg. Determined, #1567, 4½″, 1979. $15–$20

Gift box. On this hexagonal-shaped box there is a large blue ribbon on the lift-off lid, upon which Snoopy is lying. Ceramic. Deter-mined, 3″ each side, early 1970s. $55–$70

Gift box, *ceramic*. The lift-off lid is decorated with a big blue ribbon, with Snoopy and Woodstock lying on it. Determined, 4½″ x 3½″ (without bow), mid 1970s. $30–$40

Glass. This is a heavy root beer mug. Snoopy, dressed as a cowboy, is near the root beer bar and Woodstock sits atop the bar. Anchor Hocking, #3031 T–438, 7¾″, 1981. $12–$14

Heart box, *ceramic*. Snoopy is sitting on top of the white lift-off lid. Caption on lid: "LOVE." Determined, #8835, 2½″, 1977.
                                                                           $15–$18

Ice bucket, *vinyl*. Snoopy and Woodstock are dressed in formal at-tire. Black background. Shelton Ware, #9003, 1979. $75–$100

Ice bucket, *vinyl*. Snoopy, Woodstock, and a rainbow design on a white background. Shelton Ware, #9002, 1979. $60–$75

Jam jar, ceramic. Snoopy is sitting on the lift-off lid. A plastic spoon is included. Caption on front: "Jam." Determined, #8490, 4¼", 1977. $10–$15

Lunch bags. The gang, including Frieda, is shown on each of the 26 red printed brown bags in each package. Caption: "*Peanuts* Lunch Bag." Determined, #345, 1971. $8–$10*

Mustard jar, ceramic. Woodstock is sitting on top of lift-off lid. A plastic spoon is included. Caption on front: "Mustard." Determined, #1771, 3", 1977. $10–$15

Napkins, paper, beverage size. Boxed 36. Each napkin features a different comic strip. Box cover shows Schroeder, Violet, Patty, Charlie Brown, Lucy, and Linus. Snoopy with a thinner nose is sitting on his haunches. Monogram of California, early 1960s.

$25–$40*

An asterisk (*) next to a price indicates that the item comes with its original box in excellent condition. If no asterisk is shown, there is no box or the box adds little significant value. Shipping boxes (no graphics) are of no value.

A copyright date indicates the year the character first appeared in a particular incarnation, *not* the year the product first came out.

Peanut dish, ceramic. Snoopy is lying on his back on the lift-off cover. It was designed to look like a large peanut. Determined, #8824, 4″ x 7½″, 1977. $60-$75

Peanut dish, ceramic. Snoopy is lying on his back on the lift-off cover. It was designed to look like a small peanut. Determined, #8920, 2½″ x 3″, 1978. $40-$45

Pepper and salt shakers, ceramic. Woodstock is sitting on top of the pepper shaker. The holes which allow the pepper to come out are around him (3½″). Snoopy is standing and wearing a chef's hat which has holes in it, thus allowing the salt to come out (4½″). Determined, #8830, mid 1970s. Set $20-$30

Silverware baby set. Snoopy figure is on the end of the handles of the fork, spoon, and knife. The cup has a spillproof plastic cover. Leonard Silver, 1979. $25-$40*

MIB (Mint In Box): Item in unopened box, box in excellent condition.

Mint Condition: Superior quality, box missing.

Good Condition: All parts are included. Item and/or box shows limited wear and tear.

Poor Condition: Major wear and tear. Parts may be missing.

Telephone lamp. A full-figured plastic Snoopy and Woodstock stand on a plastic wood-grained base with a red platform. The touchtone dial is situated in front of Snoopy and Woodstock on the red platform. Comdial/American Telecommunications, early 1980s.

$145–$160

Thermometer for indoor and outdoor use. Snoopy and Woodstock in their dancing poses are in the center of the face. Sybron/Taylor, #5374, 11″ x 12″, 1979. $35–$50*

Toothbrush holder, ceramic. Snoopy, with a blue collar, is lying on top of a toothbrush designed to hold four toothbrushes. Determined, #8454, 7½″ x 4″, 1979. $15–$20

Tray table with snap-off tray. Depicted on the tray are Lucy, Linus, Charlie Brown, Peppermint Patty, Sally, and Snoopy standing in a group. Metal. Marshallan Products, Inc., mid 1970s. $15–$20

Tray, lap. The legs snap under to close. Snoopy appears on the tray as a tennis player, the Flying Ace, skater, baseball player, dancer, and with his hobo pack. Metal. Marshallan Products, Inc., mid 1970s. $10–$14

Tray. Cartoon panels of Charlie Brown bringing food to Snoopy and then deciding that Snoopy can get it himself. Came in various two-color combinations with black printing. Made in England. Metal. Determined, early 1970s. $20–$30

Tray. Cartoon panels. "Feed the Dog . . . and You Don't Get Thanks," says Charlie Brown. Then Snoopy kisses Chuck's hand. Came in various two-color combinations with black printing. Made in England. Metal. Determined, early 1970s. $20–$30

Vaporizer/humidifier. Snoopy lying on top of his house. Electrical. Plastic. AMSCO (a Milton Bradley Co.), #0105, 11″ × 12″ × 16″, early 1970s. $40–$60*

Walnut dish. Snoopy is lying on top of the lift-off cover. This is the companion to the ceramic peanuts dish and was designed to look like a walnut. Determined, #8921, 2½″ x 3″, 1979. $40–$45

BEDROOM ACCESSORIES FOR CHILDREN

Bulletin board. This is made of burlap, with felt appliques of Schroeder, Lucy, Charlie Brown, Linus, Snoopy, and Patty on a baseball mound. Included is a dowel and string to hang the bulletin board. Simon Simple, late 1960s. $20–$25

Growth chart. Atop chart is a stuffed Snoopy; a felt Woodstock is below him. Sixty inches of tape measure is sewn onto the felt. Directly on the felt are felt scenes of Snoopy in various activities. Simon Simple, 1972. $20–$25

Laundry bag, cotton. Full-size Snoopy drawn on the bag. He has on a red collar and a tri-cornered hat with a yellow felt flower. Red felt stars help decorate the bag. He is joined by Woodstock, who is made of felt. Caption: "1776–1976." A matching pinback button is included. Simon Simple, 1976. $25–$35

Pajama bag, Charlie Brown. Cotton. In addition to arms, legs, and eyes of felt, Chuck has a felt baseball cap, ball, and mitt. Simon Simple, 1971. $20–$25

Pajama bag, Franklin. Cotton. Has hands, legs, shoes, and lollipop of felt, but his hair is yarn. Simon Simple, 1971. $25–$35

Pajama bag, Sally. Cotton. Wears a dress with orange-red polka dots. The collar of her dress, her shoes, hair, arms, legs, and eyes are made of felt. In her hair is red yarn in the shape of a bow. Simon Simple, 1971. $20–$30

Pajama bag, Snoopy. Cotton. In his Foreign Legionnaire outfit, sports felt ears and eyes. His nose is made of black yarn. The felt flap attached to Snoopy's hat (kepi) is known as "couvre nuque" (cover neck). A pinback button captioned "Beau Snoopy" is included. Simon Simple, 1971 (see photo on previous page, bottom right). $25–$35

Pillow, felt. Snoopy is lying on top of his doghouse. Simon Simple, 13″, 1972. $20–$25

Security bag. This is an all-purpose cotton bag in red, yellow, or orange. Pictured on one side are Schroeder at his piano, Snoopy, and Sally. On the reverse we find Lucy, Linus, and Charlie Brown. In bold letters: "*Peanuts* Security Bag." Determined, #586, 24″ x 30″, 1970. $30–$35

Shoe bag. The top is in the shape of Snoopy's house. A felt stuffed Snoopy lies on top. Caption: "Snoopy" doghouse. Simon Simple, 1971. $25–$30

CALENDARS

1962, *Peanuts, A Date Book with Charlie Brown, Linus, Schroeder, Snoopy, Pigpen, Violet, and Frieda for 1962.* Black and white cover. (This was the first *Peanuts* item marketed by Determined Productions, largest *Peanuts* licensee.) Determined. $25–$35

1967, Peanuts, caption on cover. Cover design done in a psychedelic style in hot pink color. Determined. $15–$20

1968, Peanuts 1968 Date Book. Decorative border in bright colors on a black background. Determined. $15–$20

1973, Charlie Brown. Hard cardboard pressout figure. Monthly calendar pages are found under baseball glove. Determined.

$20–$30

CANDLES AND CANDLE HOLDERS

Candles

Charlie Brown. Sits with a hand on each cheek, his knees up to his elbows. Ambassador, 5¾", late 1970s. $20–$25

Charlie Brown, standing. He is wearing his traditional black pants, red shirt with a zigzag design. Hallmark, 7", late 1970s.

$10–$15

Snoopy. Wears a red and green stocking cap and sits behind Woodstock. Reverse side: Snoopy is skating. Cylindrical. Hallmark, #350CDD6583, 6″, mid 1970s. $12–$17

Snoopy, sitting with Woodstock. Lucy, Charlie Brown, Linus, and Sally are standing around. Cylindrical. Ambassador, #CDD 20R, 6″, mid 1970s. $12–$17

Charlie Brown. His baseball hat askew, he is wearing a shirt captioned "Manager." Hallmark, #325CDD7413, 4½″, late 1970s.
                    $15–$20

Lucy. Wears a blue dress and is carrying an orange-colored football. Hallmark, #325CDD7417, 3¾″, late 1970s. $15–$20

Snoopy. He is wearing a yellow tennis visor and carrying his tennis racket. Hallmark, #325CDD7416, 3¾″, late 1970s. $10–$15

CANDLES IN CERAMIC CONTAINERS

Charlie Brown, sitting with his baseball bat. The wax is located in the opening at the top of his hat and fills his entire body. Hallmark, 5¼″, mid 1970s. $30–$40

Snoopy, with his supper dish on his head. He sticks his tongue out at Lucy, making a "Bleah!" sound. Woodstock follows suit. Charlie Brown just stands by. Hallmark, 1¾″, mid 1970s. $15–$20

CANDLES IN GLASS CONTAINERS

Linus. He is pictured in the pumpkin patch. His hands are covering his mouth and his hair is standing on end. Hallmark, 2¾″, early 1970s. $20–$30

Linus, Thibault, Five, Charlie Brown, Snoopy, Schroeder, Lucy, Peppermint Patty, and Woodstock. They're all pictured in a baseball scene. Hallmark, 2½″, early 1970s. $30–$40

Candle Holders

Snoopy as a chef. He works on a layer cake captioned "Happy Birthday." Woodstock is on the side of the cake. The box is captioned "Keepsake Candle Holder." Hallmark, #1250CD8861, 2¼", 1981.

$25–$35*

Charlie Brown. Full figure and of a composition material, he is wearing his well-known baseball cap and red shirt with a black zigzag design. The candle holder portion is between his hands and off to the right. Hallmark, early 1970s. $12–$16

Linus. Full figure and made of a composition material, Linus has his thumb in his mouth and his red blanket is partially wrapped around the candle holder portion which is near his right foot. Hallmark, early 1970s. $14–$18

Lucy. Full figure and made of a composition material, she is wearing a red dress. The candle holder portion is on her left side and is captioned "The Doctor Is In." Hallmark, early 1970s. $12–$16

Snoopy. Full figure and made of composition material, Snoopy is wearing a red night cap. He holds the candle holder portion in both his hands and off to the right side. Hallmark, early 1970s. $10–$14

CLOCKS

Table alarm. Snoopy, on his tummy, is lying on his doghouse. Caption: "I'm Allergic to Morning." The case is white with a blue-green face and yellow numbers. The center colors are red and white. Metal. Equity, #596S, 4" diam., early 1980s. $30-$40*

Table alarm. Snoopy's hands tell the time. He's holding a lap flag. Woodstock in a car is the second hand. The case is white with a red face and white numbers. Metal. Equity, #592, 4" diam., early 1980s. $35-$40*

Table alarm. Snoopy as the Flying Ace with Woodstock behind him. White plastic case. Battery operated. Equity, #SN811, 3" x 2½", early 1980s. $30-$40*

Table alarm. In the center of the face of the clock, Snoopy is standing on a baseball field. His hand and bat are used to tell the time. The baseball acts as the second hand. The case is white with an orange face and white numbers. Metal. Equity, #594, 4" diam., early 1980s. $40-$45*

Table alarm. A dancing Snoopy decorates the face of the clock. His hands are used to tell the time. This style came in a variety of color combinations. Made in West Germany. Metal. Blessing/Determined, #353, 3½" x 5½", 1972. $20-$30

Table alarm. Snoopy, in his dancing position, appears on the face of the clock. His hands are used to denote the time. In the background are smaller sketches of Charlie Brown, Lucy, and Linus. It was sold in a variety of color combinations. Metal. Blessing/Determined, #355, 10½", 1972 (see photo on previous page, bottom right). $55–$70*

Table talking alarm. A three-dimensional Charlie Brown with Snoopy sleeping in his lap is on the orange plastic case. When the alarm goes off, you will hear Charlie Brown saying, "Hey Snoopy, I know you're allergic to morning. I'm losing my patience, take warning. The gang and I have places to go. Hurry, wake up, don't be so slow. We'll leave you behind good friend of mine, since happiness is being on time." Battery operated. Determined/Equity, #8002, 6½" × 6½", late 1970s. $50–$70*

Wall. In the center of the clock you will see Snoopy as a chef carrying food with Woodstock flying behind him. Caption on face: "Bon Appetit." The case is white metal with an orange face and white letters. Battery operated. Equity, #402 250, 7" diam., early 1980s. $40–$50*

COOKIE CUTTERS

Christmas, set of four. Plastic. Hallmark, #150XPF384, 1975.
$25–$75*

Charlie Brown is holding an ornament.

Linus has a string of lights.

Lucy is holding a gift package.

Snoopy, sitting and wearing an ornament that hangs from his collar.

Halloween. Snoopy on a large pumpkin. Plastic. Hallmark, #75HPF 14–6, 5½″ x 6½ ″, 1972. $75–$200*

Set of two. Plastic. Hallmark, #150XPF384, 1975. $25–$75*
  Snoopy. Thought balloon: "What's Cookin?"
  Snoopy. Thought balloon: "Hi Sweetie."

Set of four. Plastic. Hallmark, #150PF97–4, 1971. $100–$200*
  Charlie Brown with outstretched hands.
  Lucy with outstretched hands.
  Linus with outstretched hands.
  Snoopy is sitting, showing a side view.

Set of four. Plastic. Hallmark, #150PF97–4, 1971. $100–$200*

  Snoopy as the Astronaut.

  Snoopy lying on his house.

  Snoopy as the Flying Ace.

  Snoopy in his dancing pose.

Snoopy lying on his doghouse. Plastic. Hallmark, #75PF 102–3, 8″, 1973. $5–$10*

Valentine's Day, set of two. Plastic. Hallmark, #75VPF 25–3, 1974. $50–$100*

  Snoopy. A raised sitting Snoopy is inside a large heart. His thought balloon has a heart in it.

  Charlie Brown. A raised form of Chuck is inside a large heart with raised hearts all around him.

DISHWARE

Ceramic. This three-piece set has a colorful patchquilt design in the background. The 6″ bowl shows Snoopy sitting on top of his house joined by Woodstock. The rim of the plate has the names "Snoopy,

Charlie Brown, Lucy, Linus, Sally, Peppermint Patty, and Woodstock.'' The 7¾" plate has Linus sitting on a blanket with Sally,
Snoopy sitting on his house with his arms outstretched and Woodstock flying to him, Lucy jumping rope, Charlie Brown flying his
kite, and Peppermint Patty walking. The rim has the same names
that appear on the rim of the bowl. The cup shows Lucy skipping
rope, Snoopy sitting on the ground with Woodstock flying nearby,
and Charlie Brown still flying his kite. The box has an open area that
exposes the bowl. Johnson Brothers, England, for Determined, mid
1970s. $40–$50*

China. This three-piece set has a 7″ bowl that shows Snoopy in his
dancing pose, a 7¾" plate decorated with Snoopy dancing, Linus
holding his blanket while he sucks his thumb, Lucy jumping rope,
Schroeder holding his piano, and Charlie Brown as he holds a bat
with his baseball glove on it. The cup does not have any pictures,
but the names of ''Schroeder, Lucy, Linus and Snoopy'' appear near
the rim of the cup. Iroquois/Determined, early 1970s. $50–$70*

Ironstone. The design on the 12 oz. bowl and the 8¾" plate shows
Sally, Linus, Snoopy, Charlie Brown, Peppermint Patty, Franklin,
Lucy, and Schroeder each with a piece of dinnerware. Around the
picture, on both the bowl and plate, the words ''Supper and Suppertime'' are repeated. The cup shows Peppermint Patty with a glass,
Chuck with a plate, Snoopy with his supper dish on his head and a
cup in his hand, Lucy holding a pitcher and spoon. The box is captioned ''Snoopy and the Peanuts Gang.'' Taylor Smith and Taylor (a
division of Anchor Hocking), late 1970s. $30–$40*

EXTRAVAGANT SNOOPY

Handcrafted stained glass by artist Clayton Anderson (Andy Crafts, 1983, $450–$525). Mr. Anderson is responsible for the beautiful stained glass work that appears in Redwood Empire Ice Arena in Santa Rosa, California. The Arena was built by Charles M. Schulz.

Cartier-signed figural Snoopy. Snoopy standing, made of solid gold (November 1977, $5,000).

Cartier-signed figural Snoopy. Snoopy sitting, made of solid sterling silver (November 1977, $500).

Snoopy and Woodstock decorative accessory (Hallmark, 1972, $30–$40) is topped by a Snoopy Mascot Christmas tree from Japan ($50–$60). To the right is the coveted 15″ ceramic Santa Snoopy bank (Determined, early 1980s, $150–$200).

On the left is a small-size Snoopy hugging Woodstock (Determined). Ceramic wreaths (Determined, early 1980, small, $35–$45; large, $150–$175) flank paper Christmas greeting card holder (Hallmark, late 1970s, $8–$12*). Plush Woodstocks (Determined) get into the Christmas spirit.

Snoopy as Santa ($25–$35) beside tree ($45–$55). Items made in Japan.

Snoopy costumed as a skeleton (Determined) is also wearing a cloth Lucy pinback (Butterfly, 1979, $8–$10). Belle is dressed as a witch, wearing a pumpkin ring and earrings (Aviva, 1970s, $14–$18 each). They observe Halloween in a pumpkin patch made up of early 1970 Hallmark Linus ($20–$30*) and Snoopy ($15–$25*) centerpieces.

Hallmark centerpiece (early 1970s, $10–$14*) and an Easter egg decorating kit (1970s, $4–$6*) are admired by Determined plush dolls and a ceramic Easter Beagle music box (Schmid, 1985, $40–$50). Also pictured is a Lucy cardboard box (purchased in Gibraltar, $10–$15).

Top Left. Two wall posters (Hallmark, mid 1970s, $2–$3) and gift enclosure card (Hallmark, 1980s, $ .75) reflect Valentine's Day sentiments. Also pictured, Belle (Determined, mid 1970s, $8–$10), heart vase (Determined, mid 1970s, $25–$35), decorative egg (Aviva, 1970s, $8–$10), and two mini heart address books (Butterfly, 1979, $1–$1.50). *Top Right.* Happy Birthday banner from Japan ($8–$10) waves over fun party items: Linus message doll (Determined, late 1970s, $5–$8*), ceramic mug (Determined, 1970s, $8–$10), Keepsake candle holder (Hallmark, early 1980s, $25–$35*), and music box (Aviva, 1974, $30–$35).

Snoopy as Uncle Sam (Determined) wears patriotic pinback (Simon Simple, mid 1970s, $10–$15). Composition statue (Determined, mid 1970s, $25–$30*), plastic message trophy (Aviva, mid 1970s, $5–$8), Colorforms playset (mid 1970s, $4–$15), and bumper sticker (Hallmark, mid 1970s, $3–$5) all feature the Bicentennial beagle.

Right. Decorative linen towel from Scotland ($18–$25) matches Snoopy dressed as a Scottish Highlander (Determined). *Below*. Woodstock dressed in a nightie outfit (Mexico, $12–$16), Snoopy Baseball valise set (Italy, $35–$50), and plush Snoopy (Spain, $16–$25). Spike is lying on top of the sewing machine (Japan, $250–$300*), holding a red heart (Mexico, $16–$25). Woodstock guides composition rocket bank (Switzerland, $28–$35), Italian drawing toy ($30–$40*), and Hebrew *Peanuts* book (Israel, $10–$15).

Snoopy for Prime Minister decorative towel, made in Great Britain ($18–$25), Snoopy as the Beefeater (Determined), assorted children's toiletries (Great Britain, $20–$28), Snoopy cola can (Great Britain, $10–$15).

Ceramic place setting for Sushi (Japan, $50–$65).

Japanese music box ($100–$120) and piano ($250–$300).

Snoopy and Woodstock world globe ($250–$300). The writing on the globe is all in Japanese.

Japanese wooden car with Snoopy driving; the rear holds a bottle and a can opener ($150–$175). Mini set of wooden drawers ($60–$75).

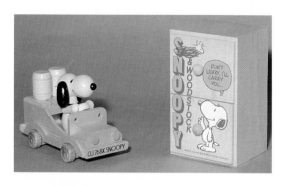

Child's kitchen set (Japan, $150–$200).

Japanese/English dictionary ($20), manual toy typewriter ($250–$300), and metal pencil cup ($8–$12).

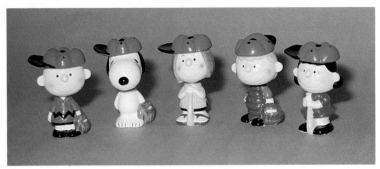

Japanese ceramic nodder set. Charlie Brown, Snoopy, Peppermint Patty, Schroeder, and Lucy ($120–$150 per set).

Inflatables from Japan include a 26″ Snoopy ($30–$40), two beach balls ($10–$15 each), and an inner tube ($10–$15). Snoopy wrapped in a beachtowel (USA, 1980s, $8–$12) can now enjoy a cool drink served in a plastic non-spill cup ($7–$9).

LAMPS

Hurricane style. Snoopy is shown dancing among the flowers. Key-type switch. White with a blue background. Kamco, 1978.

$45–$55

Nitelite/lamp. A grouping of Snoopy lying on his house, Lucy at her psychiatrist booth, and Charlie Brown sitting down. All on white base. Wood. (Original shade not pictured.) Kamco, mid 1970s.

$75–$100

Nitelite/lamp. Upper globe has hurricane lamp feature. Snoopy, Woodstock, and hearts depicted on top and bottom globes. Key-type switch. Kamco, 1978. $45–$55

Nitelite/lamp. A ceramic Snoopy holds three brightly colored balloons. Woodstock is holding flowers and standing near Snoopy. Shade: Lucy, Peppermint Patty, Charlie Brown, Sally holding balloons. On another part of the shade, Charlie Brown is flying his kite. Nursery Originals, #120–365, 18″, 1982. $35–$50

Single globe. Features Snoopy and Woodstock sitting next to each other. Six red hearts float around them. Wood stem with a metal base. Key-type switch. Kamco, 15½″, late 1970s. $40–$50

Snoopy and Woodstocks as scouts. They are roasting marshmallows. Wood. Kamco, mid 1970s. $70–$90

Snoopy rainbow. A cut-out figure of Snoopy sits in front of a pastel-colored rainbow. Woodstock is painted on alongside Snoopy. Shade: white with a yellow trim and a Woodstock motif. Plastic. Nursery Originals, #110–360, 17″, 1982. $35–$40

LUNCH BOXES

Metal, red. Charlie Brown is leaning back to pitch. Reverse: Snoopy and Woodstocks as scouts are off on a fast hike. Plastic thermos with Charlie Brown swinging his bat. King Seeley Thermos, #1448, 1976. $10–$20

Metal, tan trim. Schroeder is playing the piano while Snoopy sits on it and Charlie Brown, Linus, and Lucy watch. Reverse: Lucy, Linus, and Charlie Brown look at Snoopy as the Flying Ace sitting on top of his brown house. Metal thermos. King Seeley Thermos, #1448, 1969–1975. $10–$20

Metal, red trim. Charlie Brown sleeps against a tree while Lucy watches Snoopy kiss Peppermint Patty. Reverse: a bewildered Charlie Brown sits in front of Lucy's psychiatrist booth while Snoopy, Woodstock, and Linus look on in amusement. Plastic thermos. King Seeley Thermos, #1448, 1974. $10–$20

Metal, yellow. Charlie Brown is leaning back to pitch. Reverse: Snoopy and Woodstocks as scouts are off on a fast hike. Plastic thermos with Snoopy and Woodstock on Snoopy's house eating goodies. Charlie Brown stands in front rubbing his tummy and licking his lips. King Seeley Thermos, #1448, 1978. $10-$15

Metal, house shape in the color yellow. Snoopy is lying on his back eating a sandwich. Reverse: Snoopy is on his tummy reading a book. The metal thermos pictures Snoopy, Charlie Brown, Schroeder, Linus, and Lucy, each with their names printed beneath them. Caption on front: "Have Lunch With Snoopy." King Seeley Thermos, #658, 1968. $20-$30

Vinyl, white. Schroeder is playing his piano while Lucy leans on it. Charlie Brown and Linus are watching. Snoopy and Woodstock are dancing. Reverse side: Charlie Brown, Linus, and Lucy are playing baseball. Thermos is plastic and shows Charlie Brown swinging his bat. King Seeley Thermos, #6168/3, 1973. $25-$35

Vinyl, yellow. Binocular-style zip case "Munchies Bag" with long handle. Caption: "*Peanuts.*" Charlie Brown watches as Snoopy and Woodstock dance. Plastic thermos depicts Charlie Brown at bat. King Seeley Thermos, #6638, 1975. $25–$35

METAL TRUNKS

Footlocker. Written on each side of the lid: "Happiness is . . ." Pictured on the trunk are Sally, Charlie Brown, Violet, Peppermint Patty, Lucy, Linus, and Woodstock flying upside down while Schroeder plays his piano and Snoopy sits on it. Front: There are several pictures of Snoopy and Woodstock dancing. Left side: Snoopy and Woodstock are wrapped in a blanket holding "Rah" pennants. Right side: Snoopy lying on a smiling Charlie Brown's head. Armored Luggage, 30″ × 16″ × 12″, mid 1970s. $75–$105

Skatecase. Various poses of Snoopy, such as: Snoopy lying on his house, Snoopy as the Flying Ace, and Snoopy the golfer are printed all over. Black and white paper printed with Snoopy in various poses and outfits line the inside. Armored Luggage, 16″ x 12″ x 6½″, mid 1970s. $40–$50

PILLOWS

Determined, round, heavy cotton fabric, kapok stuffed, 16″ diam., 1971.

Snoopy, with a red cap leans on a golf club. His feet are crossed at the ankles. Caption: "You're Away." Yellow background with blue piping. #669. $10–$15

Snoopy bowling. Caption: "Strike." Green background, "Strike" in yellow. Yellow piping. #663. $10–$15

Snoopy on roller skates is wearing a blue helmet and green scarf. Caption: "Jamming." All this is on a red background with green piping. #670. $10–$15

Snoopy is kicking a green football. Caption: "The Mad Punter." This scene is on an orange background with green piping. #661.
$10–$15

RADIOS

Snoopy, Woodstock, and Charlie Brown. Characters are in a two-dimensional shape, leaning one against the other. Plastic. Concept 2000 (a Mattel Co.), #4443, late 1970s. $25–$35*

Snoopy figural radio. Shaped like a two-dimensional Snoopy. Plastic. Determined, #351, 1975. $10–$20*

Snoopy bank radio. Radio is activated by inserting a coin. Snoopy is pictured on the front, discoing. Plastic. Concept 2000 (a Mattel Co.), #4442, 1978. $45–$65*

Snoopy and a dancing Woodstock. Depicted on a two-dimensional radio shaped like a doghouse. Plastic. Determined, #354, mid 1970s. $25–$35*

Snoopy, full figure, is the radio. He is sitting on a green grass mound. Plastic. Determined, early 1970s. $35–$60*

Snoopy is pointing to the station numbers on a square-shaped radio. A microphone is included. Plastic. Determined, 1977. $50–$75*

Snoopy Doghouse Radio. Snoopy is lying on his doghouse and, if you lift him up, he becomes a handle. Plastic. Determined, #354, mid 1970s. $40–$65*

Snoopy Hi-Fi Radio. Three-dimensional Snoopy wearing earphones stands next to the orange, gray, and black radio. Plastic. Determined, #405, 1977. $35–$75*

Snoopy's Spaceship AM Radio. Shaped like a spaceship with Snoopy, a bubble over his head, sitting in it. Plastic. Concept 2000 (a Mattel Co.), #4443, 1978. $40–$80*

SWITCHPLATES

Snoopy is pulling a string attached to a light bulb. Caption: "Light Company. The Power Is On. The Power Is Off." Comes with letters so you can add your name. Hallmark, #300PF926–1, mid 1970s.

$6–$8*

Snoopy on his house as the Flying Ace. Caption: "Contact." Hallmark, #300PF929–1, mid 1970s. $6–$8*

Pigpen is surrounded by dust. Caption: "Cleanliness Is Next to Impossible." Hallmark, #300PF930–1, mid 1970s. $6–$8*

TOWELS

Linen decorator towel. Features a sitting Snoopy hugging Woodstock. Thought balloon: "A Heartfelt Apology Works Wonders!" Determined, #6390, 1976. $15–$20*

Linen decorator towel. Depicts Snoopy sitting on top of a brown doghouse receiving supper from Lucy. Thought balloon: "How Come My Kind Never Gets to Eat Off Fine China?" Determined, #6390, 1976. $15–$20*

Linen decorator towel. Pictures Snoopy sitting next to his supper dish. It is snowing. Thought balloon: "I Hate It When It Snows on My French Toast." Determined, #6390, 1976. $15–$20*

Jewelry and Watches

Jewelry made its debut in 1969 when Aviva came out with a gold-toned Snoopy Flying Ace in a pin, a tie tack, and other designs. Five cloisonné pins followed: Snoopy as Flying Ace, Charlie Brown, Linus, Lucy, and Schroeder with his piano. These were the first cloisonné-fabricated, licensed comic characters to be successfully distributed through the gift market.

A note about the cloisonné jewelry. Between 1969 and 1983 Aviva issued so many styles of *Peanuts* cloisonné—and on several occasions reissued them—that the year any individual piece first came out has little meaning. However, in many cases, we have endeavored to indicate the year a particular design was first introduced.

Most of these items were for adults. To reach the children's market with *Peanuts* designs Aviva went into hollow back pins, which were three-dimensional and considered very childlike. These pins were later replaced with flat, handpainted jewelry. Aviva also enjoyed success with their bracelets, charms, earrings, and other items of light metal, enamel, and cloisonné. Because of the superior quality of design and workmanship, coupled with reasonable prices, Aviva jewelry has become very collectible.

Despite the fact that *Peanuts* jewelry is normally of the costume variety, the famous jeweler Cartier elected to come out with a solid sterling silver Snoopy charm and an 18 karat solid gold Snoopy charm in 1977 (see color insert), neither of which is in production today. Between the appeal of Snoopy, the value of the precious metals, and the fine reputation of signed Cartier pieces, the price of these two Snoopys had no place to go but up and they have since appreciated in value many times over their original cost.

Watches are another popular *Peanuts* item. Determined introduced them in the late 1960s but it was with the ubiquitous Timex Watch Company and its large number of retail outlets (who can remember a drugstore without a Timex display?) that sales really took off and interest in watches was stimulated.

JEWELRY

Bracelets (Gold Tone)

Lucy, Snoopy, and Charlie Brown are the three charms on this bracelet. Enamel. Aviva, 1969. $25–$30

Snoopy appears in various poses. Snoopy playing tennis, baseball, bowling, surfing, and wearing a raccoon coat while holding a "Rah" pennant. Cloisonné. Aviva, 1969. $30–$35

Schroeder, Charlie Brown, Snoopy as the Flying Ace, Linus, and Lucy are the featured characters. Cloisonné. Aviva, 1969.

$35–$45

Charms

14K gold charms. Verilyte Gold, ⅝″, early 1980s.

Snoopy, sitting, holding a root beer glass. $30–$35*

Snoopy sitting on his house while Woodstock is lying on Snoopy's tummy. $30–$35*

Snoopy, sitting and holding a puffed heart. $40–$45*

Snoopy as Joe Cool $30–$35*

Snoopy in his dancing pose. $30–$35*

Snoopy as the Flying Ace. $30–$35*

Snoopy as the Flying Ace. Silver tone, is encircled in a band of silver. Aviva, 1½″ diam., 1975. $15–$20

Snoopy as a cowboy with a guitar. Silver tone, encircled in a band of silver. Aviva, ½″ diam., 1975. $10–$15

Cuff Links and Matching Tie Bar Set (Gold Tone)

Snoopy in a ski design. Cloisonné. Aviva, 1969. $35–$45

Cuff Links and Tie Tac Sets (Gold Tone)

Snoopy as the Flying Ace. Cloisonné. Aviva, mid 1970s. $35–$45

Snoopy holding an Uncle Sam hat. Cloisonné. Aviva, mid 1970s.
$40–$50

Money Clips (Gold Tone)

Schroeder at the piano. Cloisonné. Aviva, 1969. $20–$23

Charlie Brown with a baseball cap and mitt. Cloisonné. Aviva, 1969. $20–$23

Snoopy as the Flying Ace. Snoopy is flying his house. He's surrounded by clouds. Cloisonné. Aviva, 1969. $18–$21

Snoopy as The Prince. Snoopy is wearing a cape and crown. (This was made by Aviva for Interstate Brands to give to special people. Some were sold to the public by Aviva.) Cloisonné. Aviva, 1973.
$20–$30

Nifty Gifts

Cloisonné pin or earrings found inside a small paper greeting card. Look on the back for the words "Nifty Gifts." Aviva, 1⁷⁄₁₆″ x 1⁷⁄₈″, 1971–1972 (see next page for descriptions of above photo, left to right).

Pin. Snoopy holding a birthday cake. Cover: Snoopy, Woodstock, and a typewriter are on top of Snoopy's doghouse. They are holding root beer mugs. Caption: "Whee! Whooppee! WoW! Right On!" Inside caption: "Happy Birthday." $12–$15*

Earrings, for pierced ears. Snoopy bicycling. Cover: Snoopy on his house holding a letter and surrounded by red hearts. Caption: "My Heart Belongs to Only You." $12–$15*

Earrings for pierced ears. Snoopy as an English aviator. Cover: Snoopy winking. Inside caption: "Hi, Sweetie!" $12–$15*

Earrings for pierced ears. Snoopy in his dancing pose. Cover: Snoopy is kissing Peppermint Patty. Inside caption: "Happy Birthday From Someone Who Loves You!!" $12–$15*

Pins

Cardboard display. Shows a grinning Snoopy. Thought balloon: "Snoopy's Quips & Quotes Jewelry." It holds a 48-pin assortment with 12 messages. This is a type of cloisonné but of a lesser quality. Aviva, mid 1970s. Set. $120–$150

"Kiss Me Quick!"	"Junk Food Junkie!"	"Hee! Hee! Hee!"
"Hey Babe!"	"Run For Fun!"	"Why Me?"
"Bleh!"	"Hi Sweetie"	"Yawn"
"Good Grief!"	"What's Up?"	"Ah Love!"

Pin and earring set (cloisonné). Pin: Snoopy lying on top of a pumpkin. Earrings: Snoopy lying on top of a pumpkin. Aviva, 1973.
$14–$18 each

Gold tone. Snoopy as the Flying Ace. First pin produced by the manufacturer. This design was also used in a tie tac. Aviva, 1969.

$15–$20

Alphabet (cloisonné). Snoopy is designed to decorate each pin in a different pose. All initials were produced except "X," "Y," and "Z." "I" was made at first, but later cancelled. Earrings were made to match. Aviva, 1978. $5–$8 *each*

Bicentennial (cloisonné). Aviva, 1976.

Snoopy as an Indian holding a package of tea. Caption: "1776–1976." $15–$20

Snoopy is lying on the Liberty Bell. Caption: "1776–1976."
$15–$20

Snoopy is holding a flag of the 13 colonies. $15–$20

Snoopy as Uncle Sam. $15–$20

Enamel or handpainted. These pins are hollow backed and hand-painted. Aviva, 1969.

Pigpen.	$60–$75
Schroeder.	$65–$75
Linus.	$60–$70
Lucy.	$60–$70

Snoopy as an astronaut. Enameled. Aviva, 1972. $20–$25

Snoopy wearing an aviator hat and carrying a globe. Enameled. Aviva, 1970. $30–$35

Snoopy with a trombone. Enameled. Aviva, 1972. $30–$35

Snoopy with a hobo pack. Enameled. Aviva, 1972. $15–$20

Lucy wearing a blue dress. Enameled. Aviva, 1970. $20–$25

Schroeder at his piano. Enameled. Aviva, 1970. $20–$25

Charlie Brown in his baseball gear. Enameled. Aviva, 1970.
$15–$25

Snoopy in his dancing pose. Enameled. Aviva, 1970. $20–$25

MIB (Mint In Box): Item in unopened box, box in excellent condition.

Mint Condition: Superior quality, box missing.

Good Condition: All parts are included. Item and/or box shows limited wear and tear.

Poor Condition: Major wear and tear. Parts may be missing.

General assortment (cloisonné). Aviva.

Snoopy as Joe Cool is holding a frisbee. $6–$8

Woodstock holding a tennis racket. $6–$8

Snoopy holding a tennis racket. $6–$8

Snoopy, wearing a football helmet, #1 on his shirt and in a position for throwing the football. $6–$8

Snoopy swinging a baseball bat. This scene is encircled in green. $8–$10

Snoopy with a fish. $8–$10

Snoopy is on skis and Woodstock is sitting on one ski. $10–$12

Snoopy is in a raft with Woodstock. $10–$12

Snoopy with a soccer ball. $8–$10

Snoopy as the Flying Ace. $8–$10

Snoopy. Caption: "Conserve Energy." $10–$14

Snoopy is on his house with Woodstock. Caption: "Peace." $10–$14

Snoopy as the Flying Ace. Caption: "Keep 'Em Flying." $12–$16

Snoopy as the Statue of Liberty. $8–$12

Snoopy as a chef holding a birthday cake. $8–$12

Spike. 1981.	$10-$14
Schroeder at his piano.	$12-$15
Snoopy with Charlie Brown.	$8-$12
Belle wearing a red dress printed ''Belle.'' 1982.	$8-$10
Snoopy sitting in an easy chair.	$10-$14
Snoopy is lying on top of a red heart.	$8-$12
Snoopy is hugging Woodstock.	$8-$10
Snoopy is lying on top of word ''MOM.''	$8-$12
Snoopy is lying on top of a red rose.	$10-$14

Plastic. Aviva, 1972.

Snoopy in his dancing pose.	$15-$20*
Snoopy as the Flying Ace.	$15-$20*
Linus with his blanket.	$18-$23*

Snoopy is shaking hands with Woodstock.	$20-$30*
Charlie Brown in baseball gear.	$18-$23*

WATCHES

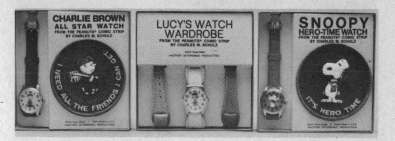

Charlie Brown All Star Watch. Charlie is dressed in baseball gear. The watch comes with a green patch of Charlie captioned "I Need All the Friends I Can Get." The face of the watch is yellow and the band is black. Determined, ⅞″ diam., early 1970s. $75–$140*

Lucy's Watch Wardrobe. Lucy is wearing a pink dress. The watch comes with blue, white, and pink interchangeable bands. The face of the watch is white. Determined, ⅞″ diam., early 1970s.

$50–$120*

Snoopy Hero-Time Watch. Snoopy in his dancing pose. Red band. Comes with round blue patch of Snoopy captioned "It's Hero Time." Determined, 1″ diam., early 1970s. $50–$100*

Snoopy Time. Snoopy in his dancing pose. Silver or gold case. Has a second hand. Available in various color faces and bands. Determined, 1¼″ diam., 1969. $45–$80*

Snoopy dancing. Woodstock is the second hand. Silver case with a red face and black band. (This dancing Snoopy is larger than those on the Timex watches.) Lafayette Watch Co., early 1970s.

$80–$125*

Lucy. Watch has a silver case and a second hand. Timex, #390141, 1″ diam., 1976. $30–$40*

Snoopy in his dancing pose. Woodstock is the second hand. The case is silver and has a red face and red band. Timex, #390151, 1¼″ diam., 1977. $30–$40*

Snoopy as the Flying Ace on his house. The entire watch and case are black. His airplane is the second hand. Clouds move around Snoopy. Timex, #84111, 1979. $45–$60*

Snoopy, standing. Silver case, blue face with second hand, and blue band. Timex, #390131, 1″ diam., 1976. $30–$40*

Snoopy in his dancing pose. Silver case, red face with second hand, and red band. Timex, #390121, 1″ diam., 1976. $25–$35*

Snoopy is playing tennis. His racket helps tell the time. The case is gold with a denim-designed face to match the denim band. The tennis ball is the second hand. Timex, #390191, 1¼″ diam., 1976.

$40–$60*

Snoopy is playing tennis. His racket helps tell the time. The case is silver and the face and band are yellow. The ball is the second hand. Timex, #390161, 1″ diam., 1977. $50–$65*

Magazines, Posters, and Other Ephemera

Ephemera refers to printed matter that does not readily fall into any other classification. Newspaper articles, magazine articles, playbills, all of them fall into this category.

To many *Peanuts* buffs, finding a good sample of ephemera or paper memorabilia is their idea of latching on to a little bit of *Peanuts* heaven. Nobody really knows everything that is out there, so coming across something new to the collector becomes very exciting—and usually informative.

A case in point is the Apollo moon landing program in 1969. Everybody knows that Snoopy was on the first moon landing. But how many people know of the extensive use that Snoopy was put to during the entire project? It turns out that our favorite beagle was an important adjunct to the program. His likeness was used in training and informational posters. A "Snoopy the Astronaut" emblem was used in conjunction with NASA's incentive award program to help keep the quality of production and the safety level high.

In the first poster to come out, which was used as an introduction to the program, you will notice that Snoopy is actually "speaking" rather than using the device of the thought balloon. The simple explanation for this is that poster makers in the 1960s preferred direct speech to the thought balloon.

Educational publication. "Urban World" is a Xerox Educational Publication. The September 29, 1972, Vol. 5 Issue 2, features a cartoon on the cover, with Violet and Charlie Brown. $14–$20

Handbook. Paramount Pictures Production Information for *Bon Voyage, Charlie Brown,* 1980. $20–$25

Lobby cards. "Race For Your Life Charlie Brown." These 14″ x 11″ cards from Paramount Pictures depict eight different scenes from the movie. $20–$40

Magazines.

Newsweek, December 27, 1971. The gang is on the cover and an article entitled "Good Grief, $150 Million" appears on pages 40–44. $8–$10

Saturday Review, April 12, 1969. The gang appears on the cover with an article entitled "The Not So *Peanuts* World of Charles Schulz," pages 72–74. $10–$15

Christian Herald, September 1967. "A Visit With Charles Schulz." $8–$10

Family Circle, May 1968. The article, "The *Peanuts* Man Talks About Children," plus pictures, appears on pages 20–24. $7–$9

Liberty, Winter 1973. The *Peanuts* characters appear on the cover and the article "Peanuts—How It All Began" is found on pages 14–16. $5–$8

Life Magazine, December 14, 1962. "On Happiness" appears on page 23. $5–$8

Life Magazine, March 17, 1967. The article "Inept Heros, Winners at Last" appears on pages 74–80. $7–$9

Newsweek, March 6, 1961. "Good Grief, Curly Hair" appears on pages 68 and 71. $8–$10

Redbook, December 1967. The cover has the gang and the article, "Charles Schulz Talks to Jack Lemmon," appears on pages 50–51, 132, 134–136. $10–$17

Saturday Evening Post, January 12, 1957. Features the article "The Success of an Utter Failure" on pages 34–35, 70–72. $15–$20

Sports Illustrated, January 8, 1968. Pages 28–34 are devoted to an article titled "That Darn Crosby." $7–$9

Time Magazine, December 14, 1962. Features an article with illustrations titled "Comics . . . Good Grief!" on pages 60–84. The cover is devoted to the gang and a little something is in the contents. $12–$15

Playbill and souvenir book.

"You're a Good Man, Charlie Brown" was shown off Broadway at the Spotlight Theatre in New York City in 1968. A playbill was given to each patron. $40–$45

"You're a Good Man Charlie Brown" souvenir book, 1969, was purchased in the theatre lobby before the show began. $15–$25

Poster. Snoopy Come Home movie poster. Snoopy with his supper dish on his head carries a hobo pack as Woodstock walks behind him. Pictured below are the other stars: Charlie Brown, Lucy, Sally, Lila, Clara, and Schroeder. 1972. $10–$12

Poster. "Join the Johnny Horizon Team—It's a Winner." This shows Snoopy with a baseball glove. Department of the Interior, #JH60 (January 1972). $15–$20

Poster. NASA. Snoopy as an astronaut heads up this poster that explains what his role will be in the Apollo space program. This information is written by one of the NASA astronauts, Wally Schirra, and bears his signature. Snoopy appears at the top of poster and is saying, "To Each Member of the Apollo Team." 17″ x 22″, 1969. $75–$100

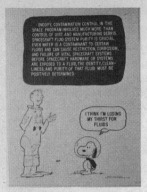

Poster. NASA. This training poster deals with spacecraft fluid system purity and contaminating properties of fluids, including water. Because of the importance and seeming complexity of this subject, Snoopy looks bewildered as he stands near a fellow astronaut and thinks "I think I'm losing my thirst for fluids." 17″ x 22″, 1969.

$50–$60

Program. "Happiness Is. . . . The 85th Tournament of Roses." This was the 1974 official program. Cover: Snoopy is holding a rose. Inside: a sketch of the Dolly Madison Float "Happiness Is . . . a Bed of Roses," which appeared in the parade. The program also featured a short article about Charles Schulz, who was the Grand Marshall that year.

$10–$15

Souvenir book. *A Boy Named Charlie Brown* souvenir books were purchased in the theatre lobby before the movie. Cover: Linus with a movie camera, Snoopy as a director sitting in a chair. Charlie Brown is wearing a baseball hat and glove and is standing on a pitcher's mound. Lucy is wearing a baseball cap and glove. Golub Bros. Concessions, 1969.

$8–$12

Souvenir book. *A Boy Named Charlie Brown* Cinema Films pressbook. Cover: Snoopy as a director holding a megaphone. Lucy, Charlie Brown, and Linus stand with him. 1969.

$20–$30

Mugs, Steins, and Chili Bowls

This group is delightful to look at and relatively inexpensive.

The mugs were especially popular during the 1970s when literally hundreds of them came out. Rather than portraying the characters, most of the mugs were embellished with scenes and bright sayings which people could relate to, such as "I think I am allergic to morning." The Christmas mugs combined all of these features with colorful scenes and lovely artwork.

Determined's annual Christmas steins, which appeared from 1975 to 1983, have become a favorite of the general public as well as collectors.

The varied and unusual shapes of many of the mugs and steins also help add to the popularity of this category. The dimensions given refer to the height of each item.

CHILI BOWLS

Ceramic

Snoopy in a cowboy outfit. Snoopy is joined by 12 Woodstocks as he heads to an open campfire to be served chili cooked by Spike. Caption: "Come and Get It." Determined, 2¾", mid 1970s.

$12–$14

Snoopy, Lucy, and Woodstock. Characters are waiting to share Charlie Brown's chili. Caption: "Wanted. World's Greatest Mug of Chili!" Determined, 2¾", mid 1970s. $12–$14

Snoopy poses in costumes from around the world. Greek, Hawaiian, Persian, Egyptian, Dutch, Spanish, and Ancient Roman costumes. Determined, 2¾", mid 1970s. $12–$14

Snoopy looking playful. Shown in eight different poses. Determined, 2¾", mid 1970s. $8–$10

MUGS

Ceramic

Snoopy is in cab of steam engine. Engine pulls two cars of celebrating characters including Linus, Schroeder, Charlie Brown, Lucy, Sally, and Peppermint Patty. There is also a small car containing gift packages. Woodstock flies overhead. Captioned in the steam engine's smoke is "Happy Birthday." Determined for the Dupont Collection Ltd., 3½", 1977. $8–$10*

Snoopy lies on top of his house. House is surrounded by sunflowers. The entire design is raised. Determined, 3¾", mid 1970s.

$10–$15

Snoopy is leaning on his gold golf clubs. Caption: "You're Away."
The scene is encircled by a yellow trim. Determined, 3¼", mid 1970s.
$8–$12

Snoopy in his dancing pose. Caption: "Come Dance With Me Baby."
The scene is encircled by a light blue trim. Determined, 3¼", mid
1970s.
$8–$12

Snoopy is kicking a green football. Caption: "The Mad Punter." The
scene is encircled by a blue trim. Determined, 3¼", mid 1970s.
$8–$12

Snoopy in tailcoat and top hat. He is presenting flowers to Woodstock. Determined, 4", mid 1970s.
$8–$10

Snoopy wears a red football helmet. He's standing in front of Woodstock. Snoopy's thought balloon: "There's Always That Chance We
Might Not Even Get Invited to the Rose Bowl." Determined, 3½",
mid 1970s.
$8–$12

Snoopy with a hockey stick. He walks in front of the net where the
puck is in the crease. Determined, 3½", mid 1970s.
$8–$10

Snoopy as a chauffeur of a Rolls Royce. He stands near the open
back door. Woodstock is the elegantly dressed passenger. Determined, 3½", late 1970s.
$6–$8

Snoopy sitting on top of his house, fishing from his supper dish.
Shermy, Roy, and Linus join in. Snoopy's thought balloon: "Find a
Good Spot and Everyone Moves In." Determined, 3½", late 1970s.
$10–$15

Snoopy is lying on the roof of his house (the red roof is the only part of the house shown). Caption on reverse side: "I'm Not Worth a Thing Before Coffee Break." Determined, 3½", late 1970s. $8–$10

Snoopy is smelling a flower. He sits in front of the large letter "F." Determined, 3½", mid 1970s. $6–$8

Snoopy is lying on top of the number "88." Determined, 3¼", mid 1970s. $8–$10

Snoopy offering a candy cane to Lucy. This forms one part of a Christmas scene that includes Linus, Charlie Brown, Woodstock, and Peppermint Patty. Caption: "Merry Christmas 1976." Determined for Joy's Inc., 3½", 1976. $8–$10

Snoopy and Woodstock are part of a Christmas scene. Other characters are Charlie Brown, who is saying "1977" as he sits with Sally. Caption: "Merry Christmas." Determined for the Dupont Collection, Ltd., 3½", 1977. $8–$10

Snoopy with his pawpets. Snoopy with Peppermint Patty, Linus, Charlie Brown, Lucy, and Woodstock are having fun around the tree. The gang is playing with toys while Woodstocks are decorating the tree with garland. Dated "1978." Determined, 3½", 1978. $8–$10

Snoopy is in a ski hat and goggles. He is carrying skis and followed by Woodstock, who is also on skis and wearing a ski hat. Reverse side is captioned: "To the Bunny Slope." Determined, 5¾", mid 1970s. $8–$12

Snoopy with Woodstock next to him. Snoopy poses as a tennis player, golfer, skier, and baseball player. Determined, 4¼″, mid 1970s.

$12–$18

Stoneware

Taylor International (a division of Anchor Hocking), 3⅜″, late 1970s.
Snoopy is sitting next to a red cup of hot chocolate with marshmallows. $6–$8
Snoopy is sitting next to a slice of cherry pie. $6–$8
Snoopy is sitting in front of a chocolate petit four. $6–$8
Snoopy as Joe Cool is standing in front of a chocolate donut.

$6–$8

Soda, Ceramic

Snoopy is holding colored balloons. Reverse side: Woodstock is holding a single balloon. Determined, 5″, mid 1970s. $20–$30

Snoopy as a soda jerk. Snoopy stands behind a soda bar captioned "Soda." Woodstock is seated on a stool with a spoon in his mouth. Determined, 5¼″, mid 1970s. $12–$18

STEINS

Dated, Ceramic

Snoopy sits on his house holding the reins to a flying Woodstock. Charlie Brown, Lucy, and Linus walk by singing. Reverse side caption: "Merry Christmas 1975." Determined, 3¾″. $25–$30

Snoopy is sitting in a red sleigh. He is wearing a stocking cap and holding the reins to a flying Woodstock. Gift boxes and yellow stars surround the duo. Reverse side caption: "Merry Christmas 1976." Determined, 3¾″. $25–$30

Snoopy and Charlie Brown proudly look at Woodstock. Woodstock flies a yellow star to the top of a decorated Christmas tree. Reverse side caption: "Merry Christmas 1977." Determined, 3¾″. $25–$30

Snoopy, as Santa, stands in front of the fireplace removing gifts from his sack. Charlie Brown is peeking out from behind a small Christmas tree. On the mantel Woodstock sits atop a plate of chocolate chip cookies while he drinks non-alcoholic eggnog. Reverse side: "Merry Christmas 1978." Determined, 3¾". $25–$30

Snoopy is sitting inside a wreath. Reverse side: "Merry Christmas 1979." Determined, 3¾". $25–$30

Snoopy sits atop his house holding a wrapped box. Woodstock, wearing earmuffs, flies in with mistletoe. There is a wreath on the side of Snoopy's house. Reverse side caption: "Merry Christmas 1980." Determined, 3¾". $25–$30

Snoopy, Peppermint Patty, Schroeder, Marcie, Sally, Linus, Lucy, and Charlie Brown are each wearing reindeer horns. They are tethered to a sled bearing a Santa Woodstock and his oversized gift sack. Caption: "Merry Christmas 1981." Determined, 3¾". $20–$25

Snoopy is standing in front of a Christmas tree decorated with red bows. Lucy is admiring a wreath and Woodstock warms himself in front of the fireplace. The scene is completed as Charlie Brown carries a holiday turkey to the table. Vertical caption: "Merry Christmas 1982." Determined, 3¾". $20–$25

Snoopy, as Santa, stuffs toys into his sack. Seven Woodstocks assist in various stages of toy making and wrapping. Caption: "Merry Christmas 1983." Determined, 3¾". $20–$25

Undated, Ceramic

Snoopy as a forlorn-looking Flying Ace. He sits at a table with an empty glass and three empty root beer bottles. Caption: "Girls and Root Beer Are Not the Answer." Determined, 5″, mid 1970s. $20–$25

Snoopy as Joe Cool. Has his arms folded and stands next to Woodstock. Caption: "Here's Joe Cool Hanging Around on a Saturday Afternoon . . . No Wheels, Man!" Determined, 4½″, mid 1970s. $20–$25

Snoopy as Joe College. He sports his raccoon coat and porkpie hat as he holds on high his "Rah" banner. He's followed by Woodstock. Determined, 4¼″, mid 1970s. $10–$15

Snoopy in nine different poses. Poses are dwarfed by the name "SNOOPY" which wraps around the stein in large yellow and red letters. Determined, 5″, mid 1970s. $20–$28

Snoopy as Joe Cool. He stands in front of a rainbow-hued arch. Caption: "Actually, We Joe Cools Are Scared to Death of Chicks." Determined, 5″, mid 1970s. $20–$25

Snoopy as Joe Cool and Woodstocks each wear shades. Caption: "Actually, We Joe Cools Are Scared to Death of Chicks." Determined, 5″, mid 1970s. $20–$28

Music
Boxes

Of all the categories of *Peanuts* collectible items that have appeared on the market, few have made a more profound impression on collectors than music boxes. Many collectors first started with music boxes. A few go no further and specialize only in music boxes. Almost all are smitten with the workmanship, the beauty, and the originality of the music box artwork.

Because of extenuating circumstances, only small quantities of two of the music boxes by Schmid got out to the stores. Consequently, their value on the after-market increased very quickly. These two are: 1) the dated 1980 Christmas box, style #289 000, and 2) a Christmas box with Snoopy, Woodstocks, and a Christmas tree, one of several to come out in 1986, style #159 101.

Music boxes first appeared in the United States in the early 1970s when Schmid imported a line of wooden boxes handcarved by the Italian craftsmen employed by Anri. Soon Schmid began manufacturing its own music boxes, both wooden and ceramic. Schmid's boxes were unique in design and sometimes added a function, such as the musical bank. Although the Aviva music boxes do not match the aesthetics of Schmid and Anri, they are rapidly gaining the attention of collectors.

With one exception, the packing of music boxes is not important to their value as collectibles. This exception is the wooden fearless Snoopy Flying Ace on top of a yellow house by Schmid (#276 762). The packaging, which consists of a color picture of the music box itself, is so beautiful that it enhances the collectible value of the music box. But buyer beware. Although this particular music box is reasonably available, finding it with the box is an entirely different matter.

Striving to obtain a complete set of music boxes can be an adventure, for they oftentimes seem to be playing hide and seek. But the joys of ownership will make the quest worthwhile for the *Peanuts* collector.

A word about dated music boxes. Schmid came out with dated Christmas music boxes in 1980, 1981, and 1982, and dated Mother's Day music boxes in 1981 and 1982. In 1983 Schmid changed its policy and issued only one dated music box for each year. They were called annuals and they were numbered and limited to 15,000. Therefore, the 1983 annual became known as the "First Limited Edition," the 1984 annual was known as the "Second Limited Edition," and so on until 1986 when Schmid ceased producing *Peanuts* items. The limited edition annuals used general themes that were not holiday related.

As we noted earlier in this guide, the themes and poses of the dated and annual music boxes closely approximated those of the ceramic plates and bells that came out at the same times. The melody played by each music box is noted in quotation marks at the end of each description.

ANRI

Wood

Linus in the pumpkin patch is shown on the cover of this musical box. Lift up the lid and there's a picture of Snoopy dancing while Schroeder plays the piano. "Who Can I Turn To." #33905/1, 6½" x 4½" x 2". $90–$110

Lucy with small mushrooms surrounding her. "Love Story." #81981, 5″, 1971. $100–$110

Lucy and Charlie Brown. They stand on either side of a mushroom taller than they are. Three smaller mushrooms complete the scene. "Rose Garden." #81973, 4″, 1971. $110–$130

MIB (Mint In Box): Item in unopened box, box in excellent condition.

Mint Condition: Superior quality, box missing.

Good Condition: All parts are included. Item and/or box shows limited wear and tear.

Poor Condition: Major wear and tear. Parts may be missing.

Schroeder at his piano. A big mushroom stands beside him and a bird (not Woodstock) sits on his piano. "Leitmotiv Kaiserkonzert." #81974, 5″, 1971. $125–$130

Snoopy kissing Lucy on the nose is the design on the cover of this musical box. A heart is over him. When the lid is opened, Snoopy is shown sitting on top of his house. "Honey." #33905/3, 6½″ × 4½″ × 2″. $90–$110

Snoopy and Lucy are next to a bird (not Woodstock.) Bird is sitting on top of Snoopy's doghouse. "Close to You." #81971, 3″, 1971. $100–$125

Snoopy, Linus, and a bird (not Woodstock.) They're standing around Snoopy's doghouse. You can see a mushroom next to Snoopy. "What the World Needs Now." #81972, 3″, 1971. $120–$130

Charlie Brown with his baseball bat. He's surrounded by little mushrooms and birds (not Woodstock). "Take Me Out to the Ballgame." #819 830, 5″, 1969. $55–$65

Linus holds his blanket. Snoopy looks as if he's planning to snatch it. Little mushrooms complete the scene. "Release Me." #819–040, 5″, 1969. $55–$65

Lucy stands behind her psychiatrist booth. "Try to Remember." #819 400, 6½″, 1969. $125–$135

Lucy stands behind her psychiatrist booth. Charlie Brown receives counseling. "Try to Remember." #819 200, 9″, 1969. $200-$275

Schroeder at his piano. Bust of Beethoven on top. There is a little bird near the piano, but it is not Woodstock. "Beethoven's Emperor's Waltz." #819 030, 5″, 1971. $125-$130

Snoopy, wearing a stocking cap, is playing ice hockey. A bird (not Woodstock) and two mushrooms decorate the scene. "My Way." #819 070, 5″, 1969. $55-$65

Snoopy as the World War I English Flying Ace on the battlefield. "Pack Up Your Troubles." #819 010, 5", 1969. $55–$65

Snoopy is ice skating. A bird (not Woodstock), a small snow-topped tree, and some mushrooms decorate the scene. "Skater's Waltz." #819 050, 5", 1969. $55–$65

Linus is in the pumpkin patch. This is a very different music box. It hangs on the wall. Turn the knob located in front to activate the music. "Who Can I Turn To." #72393/1, 6" x 8¼", early 1970s. $130–$170

AVIVA

Ceramic

Snoopy, wearing a nightcap, is lying inside a half moon. Woodstock is on the outside of the moon. Stars decorate the base. "Impossible Dream." 6", 1974. $65–$75

Snoopy holding a tennis racket in one hand and a ball in the other. Woodstock is sitting on the racket. "Lara's Theme." 7½", 1982. $30–$40

Snoopy *has his supper dish on his head.* A hobo pack is over his shoulder. Woodstock walks next to him. "Born Free." 6", 1974.

$65–$75

Snoopy *on skis.* Plain base plays "Edelweiss." Printed base captioned "Ski Love" and it plays "Edelweiss." 5¼", 1973.

$30–$35

Snoopy is wearing roller skates and earphones. Woodstock, behind him, is wearing roller skates. "Für Elise." 5″, 1982. $30–$45

Snoopy is sitting in front of his house holding a pink heart. Woodstock is on the roof of the house. Some boxes play "Love Story" while others play "Let's Fall in Love." 5″, 1982. $50–$60

Snoopy and Woodstock are wrapped in a blanket. Woodstock holds a paper pennant captioned "Rah." Base captioned "State College University." "Raindrops Keep Falling on My Head." 5″, 1973.

$25–$30

Snoopy, hugging Woodstock, sits on a removable red heart-shaped lid. The heart-shaped white base is captioned "Love" with a red heart on either side of the word. Inside it reads "And Kisses." "Love Makes the World Go Round." #215, 1982. $45–$55

Snoopy is lying on his house. Woodstock is sitting on Snoopy's tummy. This scene is set on a round base decorated with flowers. "Für Elise." 5½", 1982. $30–$40

Snoopy is on a swing. Swing is situated between two trees. Woodstock is in a nest in the tree. "Yellow Bird." 6", 1974. $60–$75

Snoopy is lying on the roof of his house. Roof is a removable lid. Woodstock is standing on Snoopy's tummy. "Candy Man." #214, 8", 1979. $45–$55

Snoopy is wearing a top hat, black tie, and carrying a cane. Manufacturer calls him Joe Class. Some boxes play "Pennies From Heaven" and some play "Happy Days Are Here Again." #213, 7½", 1979. $50–$60

Snoopy and Woodstock. They're lying down on top of the different colored letters that spell "Love" in a circular design. The bases were made two ways. Hearts on the base, "Love Story." Flowers on the base, "Love Story." 5¼", 1974. $25–$30

Snoopy is wearing a party hat and holding a birthday cake. Cake has one candle on it. Base was made in two designs: Plain base, "Happy Birthday." Base decorated with musical notes and captioned "Happy Birthday"; it too plays "Happy Birthday." 5¼", 1974. $30–$35

Composition Material

Snoopy, ceramic, is playing the concertina. A ceramic Woodstock revolves on a magnet and spins around when the music plays. "I'd Like to Teach the World to Sing." 4½" x 6", 1975. $40–$50

Snoopy, ceramic, is playing the mandolin. A ceramic Woodstock revolves on a magnet when the music plays. "It's a Small World." 4¼" x 6¼", 1975. $40–$50

Woodstock, ceramic, is sitting on top of Snoopy's snow-topped house. Snoopy, ceramic, is attached to a magnet and revolves as the music plays. "Skater's Waltz." 4¼" x 6¼", 1975. $40–$50

Woodstock, ceramic, is in a tree. A ceramic Snoopy revolves on a magnet as the music plays. "Small World." 4¼" x 6¼", 1975.
                                                                        $40–$50

Plastic

Snoopy is riding a carousel horse and Woodstock is riding a star. This is depicted on the lid of a round box with a blue background. Featured around the bottom half of the box, riding on carousel horses, are Marcie, Linus, Lucy, Schroeder, Snoopy with a cowboy hat in his hand, Woodstock flying upside down, and Charlie Brown, who fell off his horse. "Für Elise." #211001, 3½" diam. x 2½" h., 1982. $35–$45

Snoopy appears as an orchestra conductor on the lid of this round box. Woodstock stands near him playing the violin. On the bottom half, Sally, Marcie, Snoopy, Charlie Brown, Schroeder, Lucy, Linus, and Woodstock each play different instruments. "Music Box Dancer." #211002, 3½" diam. × 2½" h., 1982. $35–$45

Wood

Pasted-on picture of a desert scene on lid. Picture depicts Snoopy shown as a cowboy and Woodstock sitting on a cactus outfitted as an Indian. "Oh, What a Beautiful Morning." 4¼" x 3¼" x 2¼", 1975. $25–$35

Snoopy, ceramic, revolves on top of a piano-shaped box. A drawn picture of Woodstock is depicted playing the piano. The music plays when the drawer is opened. "Sound of Music." 5⅞" x 5½" x 6", 1974. $45–$60

Snoopy, ceramic, plays the banjo. He sits on the lid of this revolving picture frame. "Candy Man." 3¼″ x 6½″, 1974. $30–$35

Snoopy, ceramic, revolves on top of this box. The top also features a picture of Woodstock sleeping in a bed. The front is decorated with lots of drawn Woodstocks. The drawer pulls out. "Beautiful Dreamer." 5½″ x 4″ x 3½″, 1974. $50–$60

Snoopy, ceramic, revolves on top. A picture of Woodstock flying a kite decorates the lid that opens to reveal a jewelry box. The front scene shows Charlie Brown pulling a kite with Snoopy tied up in the string. "Pennies From Heaven." 7½″ x 4½″ x 3″, 1974.

$45–$55

QUANTASIA

Ceramic

Snoopy, with a trumpet, stands next to a musical note. "Für Elise." #141017, 1984. $30–$40

Snoopy sits by his typewriter as Woodstock sits on it. The base is captioned "Love is Sharing." "Feelings." #141014, 1984 (see photo on previous page, bottom right). $30–$40

Snoopy, hugging Woodstock, sits on a big red heart. Some play "Swan Lake" and others play "Let Me Call You Sweetheart." #141018, 1984. $30–$40

Snoopy is holding flowers behind him. He faces Woodstock, who is sitting in a tree. "Yesterday." #141016, 1984. $35–$40

Snoopy plays the bass fiddle. Woodstock plays the horn. "Feelings." #141015, 1984. $35–$40

Fabric

Belle, in an aerobic pose, turns when the music plays. Caption on base: "Snoopy." "It's a Small World." #141005, 1983. $25–$35

Snoopy sits on a drum holding drumsticks. He turns as the music plays. "Send in the Clowns." #141003, 1983. $25–$35

Snoopy is sitting on a square base. Base is captioned "Snoopy." He is holding a medicine ball and turns as the music plays. "It's a Small World." 1983. $35–$45

Snoopy is sitting on top of a big black hat. He turns as the music plays. "Dance of the Wooden Soldiers." #141002, 1983 (see photo on previous page, bottom center). $25–$35

Snoopy as a baby. Wears a bib and holds a bottle in his hand. Caption on base: "Snoopy." He turns as the music plays. "It's a Small World." 1983 (see photo on previous page, bottom right). $35–$45

Plastic

Snoopy is in a boat inside this waterglobe. The dome is decorated with a beach scene. The base of the globe is captioned "Snoopy." When the button is pulled out it plays "Blue Hawaii" and the boat sails around. #141020, 3½" x 2½" diam. x 2½" h., 1985.

$25–$30

Snoopy is on skis in the snow inside this waterglobe. The dome is decorated with a winter scene. The base of the globe is captioned "Snoopy." When the button is pulled out, it plays a song that no one can figure out. Maybe you can. Please let us know if you can "name that tune." Thanks. #141019, 3½" × 2½" diam. × 2½" h., 1985. $25–$30

Snoopy and Woodstock, ceramic, sit next to a raised musical note on the lid of this rectangular box. Caption on front: "Snoopy & Woodstock" with a picture of Woodstock. Comes in red or black. When the lid is opened, it plays "Für Elise." #141012, 4" × 5½", 1984. $25–$35

Snoopy, ceramic, is sitting on his house. Woodstock is sitting on Snoopy's tummy. When the roof of the house is opened, it plays "Home Sweet Home." #141013, 3" × 6", 1984. $30–$40

Snoopy, ceramic, is sitting on the lid holding a musical note. Front captioned "Snoopy & Woodstock" with a picture of Woodstock. This round box comes in red or black. "Music Box Dancer." #141011, 4½", 1984. $25–$30

Snoopy and Woodstock decorate the lid by sitting and playing music on glasses of water. "Snoopy" is captioned on the front of the base. This oval box comes in brown or wine color. "The Way We Were." #141022, 4¼" × 3" × 2¼", 1985. $20–$25

Snoopy and Woodstock appear with musical notes on the lid. The front is captioned "Snoopy & Woodstock." This oval box comes in brown or wine color. "Yesterday." #141022, 4¼" x 3" x 2¼", 1985.

$20–$25

Snoopy, raised, and a painted-on Woodstock appear on the lid, Woodstock is sitting on a musical note. The base of the box is captioned "Snoopy." Open the lid and it plays "It's a Small World." 3½" x 2", 1985.

$25–$35

Snoopy, raised, is holding a raised musical note. He is surrounded by colored musical notes. This scene decorates the lid. The base is captioned "Snoopy." It comes in red or blue. When the lid is opened, it will play "Für Elise." 3½" × 2", 1985.

$25–$35

SCHMID

Annuals, Ceramic

Schroeder at his piano. Snoopy stands on top dressed as a ringmaster. Titled: "In Concert." First limited edition. Numbered to 15,000. "Emperor Beethoven's Piano Concerto." #289–030, 6", 1983.

$50–$60

An asterisk (*) next to a price indicates that the item comes with its original box in excellent condition. If no asterisk is shown, there is no box or the box adds little significant value. Shipping boxes (no graphics) are of no value.

A copyright date indicates the year the character first appeared in a particular incarnation, not the year the product first came out.

Snoopy and Woodstocks are hiking. Titled: "Snoopy and the Beagle-scouts." Second limited edition. Numbered to 15,000. "Whistle a Happy Tune." #289-051, 7″, 1984. $50–$60

Snoopy as the Lion Tamer with Woodstock pretending to be the Lion. Titled: "Flyin' Tamer Snoopy." Fourth limited edition. Numbered to 15,000. "Pussycat, Pussycat." #289 053, 6″, 1986. $50–$60

Snoopy is lying on top of hood of the car. In the car, dressed as clowns, sits Sally, Charlie Brown, Lucy, Schroeder, Marcie, and Peppermint Patty. Woodstock sits on the rear fender. Titled: "Clown Capers." Third limited edition. Numbered to 10,000. "Be a Clown." #289 052, 5¾″, 1985. $55–$70

Charlie Brown sits holding a gift box between his feet. "Joy to the World." #417–001, 5″, 1985. $40–$50

Snoopy, *wearing a red and green hat with a matching scarf, sits with a gift box beside him.* "We Wish You a Merry Christmas." #253–721, 5″, 1984. $40–$50

Lucy *as an angel holds a book of carols.* "Silent Night." #253–722, 6″, 1984. $40–$50

Snoopy *dressed as Santa Claus with his gift sack.* Woodstock is holding a gift box and twirls when the music plays. "Here Comes Santa Claus." #418–001, 5″, 1985. $50–$60

Snoopy *dressed as Santa Claus.* He goes in and out of the chimney as the music plays. "Up on the House Top." #253–723, 6″, 1984. $55–$70

Snoopy *as Santa Claus holds a gift box.* He stands in front of his decorated house. Woodstock is wearing a Santa hat and is sitting on the roof of Snoopy's house. "Deck the Halls." #417 005, 5¾″, 1986. $35–$45

Snoopy, Sally, Woodstock, Linus, Lucy, and Charlie Brown *revolve around the Christmas tree as the music plays.* "Joy to the World." #253 724, 8", 1984. $110–$135

Snoopy is holding a star. While on the shoulders of Lucy and Charlie Brown, he attempts to place it on the top of the Christmas tree. "We Wish You a Merry Christmas." #417–004, 7", 1986. $60–$75

Snoopy *is standing next to a Christmas tree decorated with lots of* Woodstocks. "O Tannenbaum." #159 101, 7½", 1986. $250–$300

Christmas Theme, Ceramic, Dated

Snoopy is watching Woodstock. Woodstock sits in his nest up in a tree decorated with stockings. Caption: "Christmas 1980." "O Tannenbaum." #289 000, 7½", 1980.　　　　　$135–$150

Mother's Day, Ceramic

Snoopy as the Flying Ace is on top of his house. The base is a cloud and is captioned "Mom." On the back it reads "For Mother 1981." Limited to 10,000. Numbered. "It's a Small World." #289 020, 7½", 1981.　　　　　$55–$65

Snoopy and Woodstock are looking at directional signs. Signs say "Mom" in different languages. Caption on back: "For Mother 1982." Limited to 10,000. Numbered. "Edelweiss." #289-021, 7", 1982.

$55–$70

Musical Banks

CERAMIC

Charlie Brown's face is on the front. When a coin is put in the slot on top, it activates the music. "I'd Like to Teach the World to Sing." #278 041, 5″ x 4½″, 1973. $65–$85

Snoopy's face is on the front. Put a coin in and it activates the music. "Superstar." #278 040, 5″ x 4½″, 1973. $65–$85

Linus's face is on the front. Put a coin in and it activates the music. "If I Were a Rich Man." #278 043, 5″ x 4½″, 1973. $65–$85

Lucy's face is on the front. Insert a coin and it activates the music. "Second Hand Rose." #278 042, 5″ x 4½″, 1973. $65–$85

WOOD

Snoopy is inside a mailbox. Snoopy peeks out and then he kisses Charlie Brown. Woodstock is sitting on top of the mailbox. The coin box is behind the ferris wheel. The ferris wheel seats Lucy, Charlie Brown, Woodstock, Peppermint Patty, Linus, and Franklin. When a coin is inserted, the box plays "Spinning Wheel" and the ferris wheel spins around. #277 408, 8″, 1972.   -$150–$175

Snoopy dances in front of his orange house when a coin is inserted. At this time the music begins to play. You can see Woodstock sitting on top of the doghouse. "We've Only Just Begun." #277–353, 6½", 1973. $80–$100

Snoopy is lying on the roof of his orange house with a curious look on his face. When you push his tail, the music plays and the door opens. Woodstock comes out carrying a tray on which you place the coin for him to carry inside. "Raindrops Keep Falling on My Head." #276-761, 6½", 1971. $75–$95

Various Themes

CERAMIC

Charlie Brown is wearing a baseball glove and hat. "School Days." #281 019, 6¼", 1985. $40–$50

Charlie Brown, sitting. "You've Got a Friend." #253 702, 12", 1984. $175–$200

Charlie Brown, sitting. "Somebody Loves Me." #253 705, 5¾", 1984. $40–$50

Lucy, sitting. "My Favorite Things." #253 701, 12″, 1984.

$175–$200

Lucy, sitting. "Everbody Loves Somebody." #253 703, 5½″, 1984.

$40–$50

Lucy is on roller skates. "Playmates." #281 018, 6¼″, 1985.

$40–$50

Snoopy, sitting. "I'd Like to Teach the World to Sing." #253 700, 12″, 1984.

$175–$200

Snoopy, sitting. "When the Saints Come Marching In." #253 704, 5¾″, 1984.

$40–$50

Snoopy, wearing a party hat, sits on top of an opened gift box. A smiling Charlie Brown sits next to him. Caption on base: "Happy Anniversary 1950-1980." Limited to 15,000. Numbered. "Anniversary Waltz." #289 090, 6¼″, 1980. $60–$80

Snoopy is painting a portrait of himself. "I Whistle a Happy Tune." #253–000, 6″, 1986. $40–$50

MIB (Mint In Box): Item in unopened box, box in excellent condition.

Mint Condition: Superior quality, box missing.

Good Condition: All parts are included. Item and/or box shows limited wear and tear.

Poor Condition: Major wear and tear. Parts may be missing.

Snoopy and Woodstock, each on their own set of skis. They rock back and forth on the hill as the music plays. "Let it Snow." #253-720, 6", 1985. $50-$60

Snoopy as the Easter Beagle. "Easter Parade." #281 010, 7½", 1985. $40-$50

Snoopy wears a bib that says "Baby." Comes with pink or blue accents. Number given is for blue. "Brahm's Lullaby." #281 017, 5", 1985. $35-$45

Snoopy is pushing a flower cart. Woodstock twirls on top of the umbrella when the music plays. "Younger Than Springtime." #253-707, 7½", 1984. $55-$65

Snoopy is wearing a party hat and holding two pink balloons. "Up, Up and Away." #253 730, 7¾", 1985. $45-$55

Snoopy as the Flying Ace is in a red plane. The propellor of the plane is used to wind up the music. "Around the World in 80 Days." #253 729, 5¼", 1985. $45–$55

Snoopy and Woodstock on a sleigh. Sleigh rocks back and forth (as if it is going down hill) when the music plays. "Winter Wonderland." #417 000, 5½", 1985. $50–$60

Snoopy is lying on his house. Woodstocks encircle the house. When the music plays, the house revolves clockwise and the base with Woodstocks revolves counterclockwise. "Oh What a Beautiful Morning." #253 708, 7", 1985. $50–$60

Snoopy as an "Irish" Joe Cool. "With a Little Bit of Luck." #281 011, 7", 1985. $40–$50

Snoopy wears a straw hat and sits at the piano. Woodstock, wearing a matching hat, sits on top of the piano and revolves as the music plays. "The Entertainer." #253 732, 5½", 1985. $55–$65

Snoopy is dressed as an engineer holding a toy locomotive. "I've Been Working on the Railroad." #253 728, 5½", 1985. $40–$50

Snoopy dressed as a clown. He goes in and out of a gift box as the music plays. "Be a Clown." #253 731, 6½", 1985. $55–$70

Snoopy dressed as a clown. He goes in and out of a pastel-colored drum as the music plays. Woodstock is on the side of the drum. "Put On a Happy Face." #253 733, 7", 1985. $55–$70

Snoopy is lying on top of his house. "Home Sweet Home." #253 734, 5", 1985. $40–$50

Snoopy sits on a swing inside a half moon. Animated. "Twinkle, Twinkle Little Star." #281 020, 7", 1985. $40-$50

Snoopy is wearing a white nightgown with pastel stripes. His night-cap is pink. He is holding a teddy bear. "My Favorite Things." #253 726, 6½", 1985. $40-$50

Snoopy and Woodstock are on a seesaw. Seesaw moves up and down as the music plays. "Playmates." #253 709, 7", 1984. $55-$65

Schroeder *is at the piano.* The base revolves as the music plays. "I'd Like to Teach the World to Sing." #253 015, 4", 1974. $75–$95

Lucy *is wearing a blue dress.* The base revolves as the music plays. "My Way." #253 014, 4", 1974. $75–$95

Linus *is holding his blanket.* The base revolves as the music plays. "Tie a Yellow Ribbon." #253 016, 4", 1974. $75–$95

Charlie Brown *is wearing his baseball hat.* He carries his ball and glove. The base revolves as the music plays. "Impossible Dream." #253 013, 4", 1974. $75–$95

Snoopy, Woodstock, *and* Belle *are ice skating.* As the music plays, they each twirl around. "Skater's Waltz." #253 700, 4¾", 1984.

$55–$65

Snoopy as the Flying Ace has his face pictured on this musical decorator mug. It plays when you pick it up and stops when you put it down. "Fly Me to the Moon." #276 787, 4¼", 1971. $45–$55

Charlie Brown's face is pictured on the musical decorator mug. Pick it up and it plays. Put is down and it stops. "Take Me Out to the Ball Game." #276 789, 4¼", 1971. $45–$55

Lucy's face is pictured on the musical decorator mug. It plays when you pick it up and ends when you set it down. "Honey." #276 788, 4¼", 1971. $45–$55

WOOD

Snoopy and Woodstock in dancing pose decorate the lid of this box. The background flag design is in colors of red, white, and blue. Snoopy's thought balloon: "America You're Beautiful." When you lift the lid, it plays "God Bless America." #277 430, 4¼" × 3" × 2⅜", 1972. $85–$95

Schroeder, Lucy, Charlie Brown, Patty, Linus, and Snoopy are on a baseball mound which is pictured on the lid of the box. When the lid is opened it plays "Take Me Out to the Ball Game." #277–426, 4½" × 3" × 2⅜", 1972. $75–$85

Snoopy, Charlie Brown, and Linus are pictured on the lid of this box. Charlie Brown is saying, "Who Else Do You Know Who's [sic] Dog Has Just Been Promoted to Head Beagle?" When the lid is lifted it plays "Camelot." #277 421, 4¼" × 3" × 2⅜", 1972. $80–$90

Snoopy is at the end of the theatre ticket line. Sally is in front of him and behind Linus. Sally says, "You Know What I'm Doing, Linus? I'm Pretending That You're Taking Me to the Movies . . ." Linus replies "Well, I'm NOT! We Just Happen to Be Standing in the Same Line!" Patty is first on line and is paying for her ticket. Franklin is behind her. #277 427, 4¼" x 3" x 2⅜", 1972.

$100–$110

The Red Baron in his airplane. "Auf Wiedersehen." This music box does not feature any of the *Peanuts* characters, yet it is considered as a compliment to Snoopy as the Flying Ace in his green airplane. The copyright is by Schmid, not United Feature Syndicate. #276 759, 5½″, 1971. $70–$85

Snoopy as the Flying Ace in his green airplane. "When the Saints Come Marching In." #276 759, 5½″, 1971. $150–$175

Snoopy as the Flying Ace sits on top of his yellow house. "Over There." #276 762, 8″, 1971. $40–$125*

Snoopy as the Flying Ace on top of his green doghouse. When the music begins to play, Snoopy goes in and out of the roof. "Both Sides Now." #277–352, 6½", 1973. $90–$100

Snoopy as an astronaut. Snoopy is on top of a white doghouse decorated with an American flag on the side. "Fly Me to the Moon." #276 764, 8", 1971. $50–$60

Ornaments

It is universally understood that ornaments were created for one purpose—to grace the Christmas tree. This is not to say that all ornaments have a Christmas theme. They just look so darn good on a Christmas tree! Some of the more beautiful *Peanuts* sets, such as the International and Musician series, are very much in demand, admired by one and all for their quality and detail.

Most of Determined's ornaments, although sold individually, were issued by their maker as part of a series based on a theme. Naturally, collectors strive to accumulate the complete set. Ornaments, therefore, become a good example of the argument that the whole is sometimes worth more than the sum of its parts.

However, since it would be unusual for a complete set to be offered for sale at one time in an auction or market, we are pricing each item individually. We will leave it to the collector who is fortunate enough to find a complete set to decide how much of a premium should be paid for the convenience of instant ownership of the entire set.

CHRISTMAS

Balls, Dated, Plastic

Panorama ornament. This is the first of the five limited editions series, titled "Ice Hockey Holiday" and dated 1979. Snoopy and Woodstock are playing hockey. Woodstock stands on the puck. "1979" is written on a sign in front. Hallmark, #900QX141-9, 1979. $125-$175*

Panorama ornament. The second of the five limited edition series, titled "Ski Holiday" and dated 1980. Snoopy is on skis and Woodstock is going downhill in Snoopy's supper dish. "1980" is written on the banner. Hallmark, #900QX154-1, 1980. $80-$100*

Panorama ornament. The third of the five limited edition series, titled "Snoopy and Friends" and dated 1981. Snoopy is in a sleigh being pulled by three Woodstocks and it passes a snowman that looks like Snoopy. On a flake in the snow is written "1981." Hallmark, #1300QX480-3, 1981. $55-$70*

Panorama ornament. Fourth of the five limited edition series, titled "Snoopy and Friends" and dated 1982. Snoopy is in a horse-drawn type of sleigh led by six Woodstocks. They are about to take off from the chimney. "1982" is written at the bottom of the chimney. Hallmark, #1300QX480-3, 1982. $55-$70*

Panorama ornament. The fifth and final issue of the five limited edition series, titled "Santa Snoopy" and dated 1983. Snoopy, as Santa, is next to a sack of toys. Woodstock is wearing a red stocking hat and holds a streamer that is captioned "1983." Hallmark, #1300QX416-9, 1983. $45-$60*

Dated, Satin

White satin ball. Snoopy is tangled up in the tree lights. Linus is carrying two gift boxes and Lucy and Charlie Brown are on either side of a snowman. To complete the continuous scene, there is a decorated tree and Woodstock dressed as Santa Claus sitting on a gift box. Dated 1977. (Box is shaped like Snoopy's house.) Hallmark, #350QX135–5, 1977. $30–$60*

White satin ball. Snoopy, Sally, Marcie, Charlie Brown, Pigpen, Schroeder, Lucy, Woodstock, and Peppermint Patty sing "Joy to the World." The continuous scene is completed by Linus holding a wreath dated "1978." (Box is shaped like Snoopy's house.) Hallmark, #350QX205–6, 3¼" diam., 1978. $30–$50*

White satin ball. Snoopy is giving candy canes to Woodstocks who use them to decorate the tree. The caption "Merry Christmas 1979" completes the continuous scene. Hallmark, #350QX202–7, 3¼" diam., 1979. $25–$45*

Flat, Ceramic

Snoopy and Woodstock, Assortment 1. Determined, #1720, six in a set, 3", circa 1978.

Snoopy is carrying Woodstock who is sitting on a green package. #1721. $14–$18

Snoopy is holding a nest containing Woodstock and a Christmas tree. #1722. $14–$18

Snoopy is wearing a Santa suit and cap. #1723. $14–$18

Snoopy holds a red and green striped candy cane. #1724.
$14–$18

Snoopy, wearing a red and green striped nightcap with a yellow tassel, is carrying Woodstock. #1725. $14–$18

Woodstock is sitting on a red package tied with green ribbon. #1726. $14–$18

Three Dimensional, Ceramic

Snoopy as Santa Claus, articulated. Determined, 3", 1980.
$30–$40

Snoopy and Woodstock. Determined, #1029, 1975.

Snoopy carries a Christmas tree over his left shoulder. $10–$15

Snoopy is holding a green wreath and a red bow. $10–$15

Snoopy is carrying a red and white striped candy cane. $8–$10

Snoopy is in a Santa suit, holding yellow bells. $8–$10

Snoopy is wearing a red Santa hat and lying on two gift boxes.

$8–$10

Woodstock is sitting on a red package with a green ribbon.

$8–$10

Vehicles, Snoopy and Woodstock. Determined, #1315, set of six, circa 1979.

Woodstock is wearing a Santa cap and driving a red fire truck trimmed in green. $15–$20

Snoopy, wearing a Santa cap, is riding a red, black, and green steam engine. $15–$20

Woodstock is driving a motorcycle with red and green packages behind him. $15–$20

Snoopy guides a blue and white boat with a red deck. A Christmas tree is in the boat situated behind Snoopy. $15–$20

Snoopy is wearing a Santa cap and riding a blue car with a green wreath on the hood of the car. $15–$20

Snoopy, wearing an aviator's cap and carrying a green sack, is in a red airplane. $15–$20

MIB (Mint In Box): Item in unopened box, box in excellent condition.

Mint Condition: Superior quality, box missing.

Good Condition: All parts are included. Item and/or box shows limited wear and tear.

Poor Condition: Major wear and tear. Parts may be missing.

THREE DIMENSIONAL
Ceramic

Adventure series, Snoopy. Determined, #1140, circa 1975.

Snoopy as a clown. #1141.	$15–$20
Snoopy as Robin Hood. #1142.	$15–$20
Snoopy as a bandit. #1143.	$15–$20
Snoopy as an American Indian. #1144.	$15–$20
Snoopy as a detective. #1145.	$15–$20
Snoopy as Davy Crockett. #1146.	$15–$20

Bicentennial. Determined, #1099, 1975.

Snoopy is playing the drum. #1096.	$20–$25
Snoopy is holding a paper American flag. #1097.	$20–$25
Snoopy is wearing an Uncle Sam hat. #1098.	$20–$25

International series. Determined, #8860, set of 12, circa 1977 (see descriptions on next page for above photo).

Snoopy as an English gentleman with bowler hat and umbrella, England. #8880. $15–$20

Snoopy is wearing a sombrero and serape, Mexico. #8862.
$15–$20

Snoopy is wearing a kimono, Japan. #8868. $15–$20

Snoopy is wearing a Venetian hat, Italy. #8867. $15–$20

Snoopy is wearing a turban, India. #8873. $15–$20

Snoopy is wearing a top hat and cape, Transylvania. #8879.
$15–$20

Snoopy is dressed as a bullfighter, Spain. #8861. $15–$20

Snoopy is dressed as an artist, holding a palette, France. #8865.
$15–$20

Snoopy as a Viking, Scandinavia. #8878. $15–$20

Snoopy is dressed in kilts and holds a bagpipe, Scotland. #8866.
$15–$20

Snoopy dressed as a Royal Palace Guard, England. #8864.
$15–$20

Snoopy in a Tyrolean outfit, German. #8863. $15–$20

Junkfood series. Determined, #1905, 1982.

Snoopy is holding a glass of root beer. $10–$15

Snoopy is lying on top of a slice of cherry pie. $10–$15

Snoopy is sitting in a bag of french fries. $10–$15

Snoopy is sitting in front of a chocolate ice cream cone.
$10–$15

Snoopy is lying on top of a hamburger. $10–$15

Snoopy is lying on top of a hot dog. $10–$15

Mascots. Determined, mid 1970s.

Snoopy, 2½″. $35–$45

Charlie Brown wearing his baseball hat, 3″. $35–$45

Musician series. Determined, #1700, circa 1976.

Linus is playing a gold saxophone. #1704. $15–$20

Peppermint Patty is playing the guitar. #1702. $15–$20

Schroeder is playing the piano. #1705. $15–$20

Lucy is playing a yellow trumpet. #1703. $15–$20

Snoopy is playing the bass violin. #1706. $15–$20

Charlie Brown is playing a red and yellow bass drum. #1701.

$15–$20

Sports. Snoopy with an orange surfboard. Determined, #1152, circa 1975. $8–$10

Sports series. Determined, #1080, 1975.

Snoopy as a tennis player wearing a visor and holding a tennis racket #1086. $8–$10

Snoopy as an Olympic runner with a 1975 on his shirt. #1085.

$8–$10

Snoopy with skis in his hand and wearing a snow cap. #1082.

$8–$10

Snoopy as a baseball player wearing baseball cap and glove. #1084. $15–$20

Snoopy as a football player wearing a red helmet and holding a football. #1083. $15–$20

Snoopy as a golfer holding a golf club. #1081. $15–$20

Pinbacks (Buttons)

People like to wear pinbacks. The slogans are pretty evenly divided between those that amuse and those that reflect on the times. Either way, they allow the wearer an opportunity to express himself or herself to anyone who happens to be nearby.

Simon Simple, in particular, is noted for the creativity of its *Peanuts* pinbacks.

Button collecting, for both *Peanuts* and otherwise, is one of the fastest growing hobbies today, which puts a lot of pressure on the demand.

"Flasher" pinbacks will change scenes by moving them slightly. The two scenes ingeniously combine together to show action and tell a little story.

Manufacturers also found buttons to be a novel way to promote their products.

AVIVA

Movee [sic] buttons. Picture changes when button is moved. Twelve designs to a set. On the back of the button is a black and white picture of Snoopy in dark glasses and standing on a director's chair, which has his name on it. Plastic front, metal back. 2½" diam., 1972–1973.

Snoopy misses a baseball pitch. Caption: "Strike One!"

$10–$12

Snoopy as the Flying Ace is diving off his house. Caption at bottom: "Aaugh!" $10–$12

Charlie Brown pitches a ball. It goes past him so fast that he turns upside down and loses his clothes. $12–$15

Charlie Brown is running toward Lucy who is holding the football. As usual, she picks it up and he goes flying in the air. He yells, "Aaugh!" $12–$15

Snoopy, wearing a red helmet, throws a football and it lands on Woodstock's head. He sees stars. Caption: "Bonk." $10–$12

Snoopy is playing tennis. A hard serve comes to him and knocks him over. Thought balloon: "I Hate it When They Serve Hard!"

$10–$12

Snoopy wears a ten-gallon hat while playing his guitar and tapping his foot. $10–$12

Snoopy and Woodstocks walking. $12–$15

Snoopy is lying on his back on the roof of his red doghouse. Snoopy sneezes and Woodstock, who was flying by his nose, ends up on his feet. Caption: "Ahchoo." $12–$15

Snoopy does some fancy steps from his famous "suppertime" dance. Autumn-colored leaves flutter by. $10–$12

Snoopy is walking behind Lucy. When she turns around, he surprises her by kissing her on the nose. $12–$15

Snoopy watches Woodstock as he flies over his head and lands neck deep in the snow. Snoopy is so surprised, his ears stick straight up. $12–$15

BUTTERFLY ORIGINALS

Charlie Brown is on the baseball mound. Caption: "Only 25 Years Old and They're Doing My Life Story!" Metal. 3¾" diam., 1975.

$20–$30

Snoopy is lying on top of a pumpkin. Cloth front, metal back. 2¼" diam., early 1980s.

$5–$8

Lucy as a witch carrying her broom. Cloth front, metal back. 2¼" diam., early 1980s.

$8–$10

Snoopy as Joe Cool is leaning up against a pumpkin. His hands and feet are crossed. Cloth front, metal back. 2¼" diam., early 1980s.

$6–$8

Snoopy is reading ghost stories to Woodstock. They both look frightened. Cloth front, metal back. 2¼" diam., early 1980s.

$5–$8

Snoopy with his famous grin is holding a bag captioned "Trick or Treat." Caption on pin: "Trick or Treat." Cloth front, metal back. 2¼" diam., early 1980s.

$5–$8

Snoopy and Woodstock. They're on top of Snoopy's doghouse howling at the moon. Cloth front, metal back. 2¼" diam., early 1980s.

$5–$8

HALLMARK

Flashers. Move the button and the picture changes. Plastic. 3″ diam., early 1970s.

Snoopy is in his dancing pose. When the button is moved it is captioned "Snoopy for President." $15–$20

Linus is in the pumpkin patch, leaning his elbows on the pumpkin. He says, "The Great Pumpkin Is Watching You." $20–$30

Schroeder is holding a sign captioned "Halloween's Here!" When the button is moved, the sign changes to "Only 40 Shopping Days 'til Beethoven's Birthday." $20–$30

PROMOTION PINBACKS

Snoopy as the Flying Ace is looking through his binoculars. This red, white, and blue pin is captioned "Butternut Bread" and "Snoopy's Spotters Club." Metal. Interstate Brands, 2″ diam., early 1970s. $12–$15

Snoopy is walking with his school books on his head. Woodstock is flying with his books between his feet. Caption: "Take Snoopy Back to School." Metal. Butterfly, 2½″ diam., early 1980s. $6–$10

Snoopy is wearing an Uncle Sam hat. Captions: "Snoopy for President" and "Dolly Madison for Cakes." Metal. Interstate Brands, 3″ diam., 1972. $8–$12

Snoopy is wearing a crown and a red neckerchief. Picture is of his head only. Caption: "The Prince of Sandwiches." Metal. Interstate Brands, 1½″ diam., 1973. $8–$12

SIMON SIMPLE

"All I Need Is One Hit and I Can Raise My Lifetime Batting Average to .001." Lucy is telling this to Charlie Brown. Metal. 1¾″ diam., early 1970s. $15–$20

"All Secretaries Need a Little Compliment Now and Then." Woodstock is on Snoopy's house typing a letter. Snoopy pats him on the head. Thought balloon: "That's Very Nice." Metal. 6" diam., early 1972 (see photo above, center). $20–$30

"Big Man on Campus!" Snoopy is wearing his raccoon coat and porkpie hat and carrying a "State" banner. Metal. 1½" diam., early 1970s. $8–$12

"Big Man on Campus." Snoopy. Metal. 1½" diam., early 1970s. $10–$15

"Curse You Red Baron!" Snoopy as the Flying Ace is on his red, white, and blue house. Metal. 1¾" diam., early 1970s (see photo on next page, top right). $10–$15

"Dogs Accept People for What They Are." Linus hugging Snoopy. Metal. 1¾" diam., early 1970s. $15–$20

Election hat with four metal buttons, which are pinned to a red, white, and blue decorative ribbon. This straw hat was manufactured for the 1972 election. $75–$90

"Snoopy for President." Snoopy with his hand over his heart. This pinback is viewable. 2½" diam.

"Vote for Lucy Diplomatic Service." Lucy with a fist. 1¾" diam.

"I Believe in Statehood, Countryhood, Cityhood and Neighborhood." Linus with his blanket. 1¾" diam.

"You're a Good Man Charlie Brown." Charlie Brown, 1¾" diam.

"Good Grief." Snoopy is playing golf and Charlie Brown is watching. Metal. 1¾" diam., early 1970s. $15–$18

"Happy Birthday America." Snoopy is wearing a tri-cornered hat. Also pictured is Woodstock and a large lighted birthday cake. Caption: "1776–1976." Metal. 1¾" diam., 1976. $10–$15

"Help Stamp Out Things That Need Stamping Out." Linus is carrying the captioned sign and walks between Lucy and Snoopy, who is just looking at him. Metal. 6" diam., 1972 (see photo on previous page, top right). $25–$30

"Here's Beau Snoopy of the Foreign Legion Marching Across the Desert." Snoopy in his Foreign Legion hat walking through the desert. Metal. 1¾" diam., 1971. $15–$20

"Here's the WW1 Pilot Flying in his Sopwith Camel Searching for the Red Baron!" Snoopy as the Flying Ace on top of his house. Metal. 1¾" diam., early 1970s. $12–$15

"I Believe in Statehood, Countryhood, Cityhood and Neighborhood." Linus with his hands outstretched and his blanket in his right hand. Metal. 1¾" diam., 1972. $8–$12

"I Don't Care if Anyone Likes Me Just So I'm Popular!" Lucy is saying this to Charlie Brown as they stand behind a low brick wall, with their elbows leaning on top. Metal. 1¾" diam., early 1970s.
$12–$15

"I Kissed a Crabby Face." Snoopy kissing Lucy. Metal. 1¾" diam., early 1970s (see photo above, left). $15–$20

"The In Crowd." Front: Sally, Linus, Lucy, Charlie Brown. Back: Frieda, Schroeder playing the piano, Violet, Snoopy, Patty, and Pigpen. Metal. 3" diam., early 1970s. $30–$40

"It Always Rains on Our Generation!" Linus and Lucy walking in the rain. Metal. 1¾" diam., early 1970s. $10–$15

"I Think My Feet Need Sharpening!" Snoopy wearing a red and black stocking cap has taken a flop on the ice. Metal. 1¾" diam., early 1970s. $12–$15

"I'm on the Moon!" Snoopy in an astronaut suit. Metal. 1¾" diam., 1970. $18–$25

"It's Good to Have a Friend." Snoopy with a bunny. Metal. 1¾" diam., early 1970s. $15–$20

"Just What a Manager Likes Is a Player Who Isn't Bothered by Tension." Charlie Brown and Snoopy, who is sleeping in his lap, are on a bench. They have on baseball hats. Metal. 1¾" diam., early 1970s. $15–$20

"Monday Is Beethoven's Birthday!" This sign is held by Schroeder. Snoopy is holding the sign captioned "Have a Good Time!" Metal. 1½" diam., early 1970s. $15–$20

"Sleeping Is an Art." Snoopy lying on top of his doghouse. Metal. 1¾" diam., early 1970s. $12–$15

"Snoopy Come Home." Snoopy, with a hobo pack and his supper dish on his head, is walking as Woodstock follows him. Metal. 1¾" diam., 1972 (see photo on previous page, top center). $5–$10

"Snoopy Come Home." Snoopy, with a hobo pack and his supper dish on his head, is walking as Woodstock follows him. Metal. 6" diam., 1972 (see photo on p. 218, top left). $18–$22

"Snoopy for President." Snoopy with his hand over his heart. Metal. 1972.

½" diam.	$8–$12
1½" diam.	$8–$12
2½" diam.	$12–$15

"To Those of Us With Real Understanding, Dancing Is the Only Pure Art Form." Snoopy in his dancing pose. Metal. 1½" diam., early 1970s. $10–$14

"Vote For Lucy For Diplomatic Service." Lucy with a fist. Metal. 1¾" diam., 1972. $8–$12

Planters and Vases

Ceramic fans had a field day with ceramic planters and vases. Their high gloss, combined with attention to detail and unique designs, made them extremely desirable. Since they were reasonably priced and sold in almost every Hallmark store and florist shop, they were also easily available. Even on today's secondary market they are not highly priced, considering the quality of the product.

Collectors might be aware that the underside of many of the ceramic planters and vases by Determined bear the initial "Z" by itself or the initial "Z" inside a circle. The "Z" stands for the Wm. Zappettini Co., which is a big distributor to florists and gift shops.

Since the "Z" mark has no influence on collectible value we did not include it in our descriptions.

GARDENING ACCESSORIES

Snoopy sits and welcomes Woodstock, with outstretched hands. Woodstock is bringing him flowers. This scene decorates the watering can. Determined, #1123, 4¾", mid 1970s. $20–$30

Snoopy is *watering the garden as Woodstock flies about.* This scene appears on the watering can that contains three gardening tools. Determined, #1119, 3″, mid 1970s. $25–$35

MINI COLLECTION, CERAMIC

Determined, mid 1970s.

Milk can. Lucy. 2″. $5–$8

Milk can. Snoopy is sitting and hugging Woodstock. 2″. $5–$8

Stein. Peppermint Patty is standing with outstretched hands. 2″.
                                                                                      $5–$8

Stein. Snoopy is sitting in front of a rainbow: 2″. $5–$8

Vase. Charlie Brown has one hand touching his chin. 2″. $5–$8

Vase. Snoopy is giving Woodstock a kiss. They are both wearing Hawaiian leis. 2″. $5–$8

MIB (Mint In Box): Item in unopened box, box in excellent condition.

Mint Condition: Superior quality, box missing.

Good Condition: All parts are included. Item and/or box shows limited wear and tear.

Poor Condition: Major wear and tear. Parts may be missing.

Determined, mid 1970s.

Kettle. Snoopy, flower in hand, is lying on the word "Snoopy." 3″.
$8–$12

Kettle. Snoopy is standing near yellow flowers. Caption: "Snoopy." 2½″.
$8–$12

Kettle. Snoopy is sitting on his name and reaching for a yellow and red flower. 2¾″.
$8–$12

Milk can. Snoopy is sitting with a horseshoe of red flowers. Caption: "Snoopy." 3″.
$8–$12

Pail. Snoopy is sitting next to a large red tulip. Caption: "Snoopy." 3″.
$8–$12

PLANTERS

Ceramic

Snoopy and Woodstock in their dancing poses are repeated around the bucket. Bucket has a metal wire handle. Snoopy is drawn in green instead of the traditional black. Caption: "Flowers." Determined, #1209, 4¾″, mid 1970s.
$15–$25

Snoopy has flowers behind his back. He looks down toward a smiling Woodstock on this cream pitcher-shaped planter. Determined, #1297, 4″, mid 1970s.
$15–$20

Snoopy appears with a different flower on every other panel on this octagon-shaped bowl. Woodstock is shown on alternate panels. Determined, #1525, 2¼″ h. x 4½″ d., mid 1970s.
$10–$15

Woodstock holds a flower as he sits on Snoopy's head. He's surrounded by lots pf pink, blue, and yellow flowers. Opposite side shows Snoopy with a big grin on his face as he waters the flowers. Woodstock flies about. Caption on both sides: "Jardinière." Determined, #1210, 3½" h. x 4¾" d., mid 1970s. $25-$35

Snoopy is pictured on a berry basket wheeling a flower cart. Cart is filled to the rim with beautiful flowers. An open umbrella protects them. Determined, #1122, 3½" h. x 4¾" w., mid 1970s. $25-$35

Snoopy, working in his garden, is pictured on the front of this pot which sits in its matching saucer. Reverse side: Woodstock is sitting among the flowers. Caption: "Woodstock is Really Into Flowers." Determined, #1208, 3¼", mid 1970s. $25-$35

Snoopy, three-dimensional. Snoopy is climbing up the white pot, which is sitting in its own saucer. Determined, mid 1970s.

#1199, 4¼". $32-$35

#1198, 3". $25-$28

Snoopy, as a vaudeville performer, stands on stage. Woodstock joins him. Snoopy is wearing a red and white striped jacket, bowtie, and is holding a straw hat in one hand and a bouquet of flowers in the other hand. Determined, #1212, 4¼", mid 1970s. $30–$40

Snoopy, full figure, is standing next to a large white barrel. Caption: "Snoopy." Determined, #1105, 6¾", mid 1970s. $35–$45

Snoopy, full figure, is standing next to a small barrel. Caption: "Snoopy." Determined, #1115, 4¼", mid 1970s. $25–$35

Snoopy is lying on the handle of a white basket. Determined, #1120, 5¾", mid 1970s. $24–$30

Snoopy is sitting and the opening in his back serves as the plant holder. Determined, #1118, 5", mid 1970s. $25–$35

Snoopy and a sunflower, both in a raised design appear on the front of the pot. Determined, #1194, 3¾", mid 1970s. $20–$25

Snoopy, sitting on the grass and hugging Woodstock, appears on the front of the pot that sits in its own saucer. They are surrounded by flowers and floating red hearts. Snoopy's thought balloon on opposite side: "Surprise a Friend With a Hug." Determined, #1195, 3¼", mid 1970s. $24–$30

Snoopy and Woodstock appear in various poses on different sized pots of similar shape. Determined, #1190, mid 1970s.

Snoopy in his dancing pose and Woodstock flying behind him. 2". $10–$12

Snoopy and Woodstock are sitting among the flowers. Woodstock holds a bunch of flowers while Snoopy holds just one. 2½".

$15–$20

Snoopy is sitting and hugging Woodstock. They are surrounded by floating red hearts. 3¼". $30–$35

Snoopy, full figure, has his supper dish on his head and Woodstock on his nose. In his left hand he is carrying a yellow valise (with a full supply of chocolate chip cookies). Determined, mid 1970s.

#1101, 7½". $25–$30

#1102, 4½". $15–$20

Snoopy and Woodstock each appear on alternate sides of this octagon-shaped bowl. Woodstock is alone but Snoopy poses with a large flower. Determined, #1197, 2¼" h. x 4½" d., mid 1970s.

$16–$20

Snoopy is lying on the roof of his house that was produced in three sizes. One side of the roof is open to permit planting. Determined, mid 1970s.

4¾", #1113. $15–$20

6¼", #1111. $20–$25

7¾", #1103. $35–$50

Snoopy is being carried through the air by Woodstock in an orange colored polka dot blanket. Three more Woodstocks are nearby. This scene is depicted on the sides of the cradle. Determined, #1293, 2½", x 3" x 3½", mid 1970s. $20–$30

Snoopy and Woodstock are depicted on the drum in different poses. In one scene, Woodstock is kissing Snoopy on the nose. An orange trim on top ends in a bow design while the bottom trim is blue. Determined, #1292, 3" h. x 3" d., mid 1970s. $25–$30

Snoopy with various objects, each representing a letter of the alphabet from A to E, is shown on the baby block. He is sometimes joined by Woodstock. Determined, #1291, 3″, mid 1970s. $15–$20

Snoopy and Woodstock are the featured characters on the baby shoe. Snoopy is wheeling a pink carriage while Woodstock flies nearby. The reverse side shows Woodstock in a baby carriage with Snoopy nearby. The baby shoe comes with blue or pink laces. Determined, #1290, 3½″, mid 1970s. $25–$35

Snoopy as Santa Claus is in front of the sleigh and Woodstock is on the back. A sprig of holly decorates the side of the sleigh. Determined, #1529, 4½″ h. x 5⅞″ l., mid 1970s. $35–$45

Snoopy, *full figure and wearing a Santa cap*. He is leaning on a chimney decorated with a wreath. Determined, #1106, 7½", mid 1970s. $50–$70

Snoopy, *full figure and wearing a Santa cap*. He is leaning on the barrel that is captioned "Merry Christmas." Determined, #1117, 4½", mid 1970s. $35–$45

Snoopy is *leaning his head over the mailbox*. On the door of the mailbox is written "Mail." Woodstock is up against the right side of the mailbox upon which "U.S." is written. Determined, #1528, 3¼", mid 1970s. $25–$30

Snoopy, *full figure, is in front of a red heart-shaped planter holding a yellow bunch of flowers*. Woodstock is on the top of the heart peeking down at Snoopy. Determined, #1530, 4", mid 1970s. $20–$24

Snoopy is *lying on top of a red and blue mailbox*. The mail schedule is printed on the front. Caption: "U.S. Mail." Determined, 3½", mid 1970s. $20–$30

Snoopy, *sitting and holding bright yellow, red, and orange flowers* is pictured on this kidney-shaped planter. A butterfly rests on the largest flower. Determined, #1917, 2", mid 1970s. $15–$20

Snoopy, *full figure*. He leans against an oblong white basket that has a handle. Determined, Snoopy: 4½″, basket: 2½″ x 4″, mid 1970s.

$25–$35

Woodstock, *full figure*. He is standing and peering into an oblong white basket that has a handle. Determined, Woodstock: 4½″, basket: 2½″ x 4″, mid 1970s.

$25–$35

Snoopy, *surrounded by Woodstocks, is carrying a green banner with a red heart on it*. This scene is depicted on the purse-shaped planter. Determined, 4¾″, mid 1970s.

$40–$50

Snoopy, *dressed as Santa Claus*. Snoopy sits with Woodstock and a large open gift sack between them. The gift sack serves as a planter. Determined, 4″, mid 1970s.

$30–$40

Snoopy sniffs a yellow flower as Woodstock looks up at him. They are surrounded by a "lace"-trimmed red heart in this heart-shaped planter with pedestal legs. Determined, 3¼", mid 1970s. $25–$35

Snoopy, as Joe Cool, in a raised design. Snoopy stands in front of a rainbow that is on the front of the rainbow-shaped planter. Determined, 4¼", mid 1970s. $25–$35

Snoopy as a cowboy. Snoopy holds a lariat and Woodstock wears an Indian feather headband. They appear in a raised design on the boot. Determined, 4¾", 1980. $20–$30

Plastic

Snoopy and Woodstock appear in three different poses. They are in front of a bright blue, green, yellow, and red rainbow. Determined, #1274, 6¾" h., mid 1970s. $15–$25

VASES

Ceramic

Linus and Sally are smiling and happy as they hold hands and walk together. Caption: "Love Is Walking Hand in Hand." Determined, #1573, 5½", mid 1970s. $25–$30

Snoopy is on his house kicking his feet and laughing. Caption: "It's Hard to Feel Sorry For Yourself When You're Happy." Determined, 7¼", mid 1970s. $25–$35

Snoopy, in a raised design, appears as if he's thinking of someone special. He is shown up against the front of the red heart-shaped vase which lies on its side. Determined, 4", mid 1970s. $25–$35

Snoopy is searching through a bookcase. On the opposite side of what appears to be an open book is captioned "Ah Here It Is, a Beagle's Blooming Garden Guide!" Determined, #1278, 3½" h. x 5" w., mid 1970s. $20–$30

Snoopy is kissing Sally. Caption: "All Girls Look Forward to Their First Kiss." Determined, #1218, 5½", mid 1970s. $25–$35

Snoopy is sitting among the flowers. Caption: "How Nice" appears on this cylinder-shaped vase. Determined, #1281, 7¾", mid 1970s.
                                                   $22–$30

Snoopy, *standing and wearing a blue and gold badge*. Captioned "Hero" in red lettering. Snoopy lends his shape to the vase, which is flat in both the front and back. Determined, #1127, 7″, mid 1970s. $30–$40

Snoopy *stands on a patch of lawn*. He holds red, yellow, and blue balloons, as shown on the front of the bud vase. Determined, #1124, 6½″, mid 1970s. $30–$40

Snoopy, *raised and wearing a badge captioned "Hero" on his chest*. He is in front of this yellow star-shaped vase. Determined, #1126, 4¼″, mid 1970s. $20–$30

An asterisk (*) next to a price indicates that the item comes with its original box in excellent condition. If no asterisk is shown, there is no box or the box adds little significant value. Shipping boxes (no graphics) are of no value.

———————

A copyright date indicates the year the character first appeared in a particular incarnation, *not* the year the product first came out.

Snoopy is lying on his house. A sunflower is growing right over him. Thought balloon: "All Right, Who Planted the Flower?" Cylindrical shape. Determined, #1283, 8½", mid 1970s. $35–$45

Snoopy is sitting and holding flowers to his nose. The yellow background is dotted with small flowers and framed by a green oval. Determined, 7¼", early 1970s. $20–$25

Snoopy is sleeping on the roof of his house. Woodstock is sleeping in a nest that is on Snoopy's tummy. Caption on the back of this bud vase: "This Has Been a Good Day." Determined, #1128, 5", mid 1970s. $20–$30

Glass

Snoopy as a cowboy. He wears a pained expression as he lies near a water fountain in the desert. Woodstock flies toward him. Caption: "Nothing Is as Easy as It Looks." Anchor Hocking, 6¾", 1978.

$8–$12

Snoopy is playing the guitar and singing to Woodstock. Caption: "There's a Little Bit of Country in All of Us." Anchor Hocking, 6¾", 1978. $8–$12

Snoopy is prancing about and throwing flowers to Woodstock. Caption: "Love Drives Me Crazy." Anchor Hocking, 6¾", 1978.

$8–$12

Snoopy, in a tuxedo and top hat, is giving flowers to Woodstock. Caption: "To You, My Special Friend." Anchor Hocking, 6¾", 1978. $8–$12

Snoopy is being carried by Woodstock, who is imitating a stork. Other Woodstocks are flying around. Caption: "Congratulations." All on a pink background with blue lettering. Anchor Hocking, 6¾", 1978. $8–$12

Snoopy kicks up his bandaged leg. Caption: "Get Well Soon." This is depicted on a yellow background with blue lines that form squares. Anchor Hocking, 6¾", 1978. $8–$12

Snoopy, Lucy, and Peppermint Patty admire baby Woodstock lying in the cradle. Pink, blue, and white background. Caption: "What a Cutie." Anchor Hocking, 6¾", 1978. $8–$12

Snoopy and Woodstock don their party hats as they get ready to share a birthday cake. Blue background with gold trim. Caption: "Happy Birthday." Anchor Hocking, 6¾", 1978. $8–$12

Snoopy has flowers brought to him by Woodstock. This is on a red, blue, and gold background. Caption: "How Nice." Anchor Hocking, 6¾", 1978. $8–$12

Snoopy, wearing a Santa hat and holding a candy cane. He is pictured with Woodstock, who is seated on a green gift box. Yellow stars border the red background. Anchor Hocking, 6¾", 1978.
$10–$15

Snoopy is hugging Woodstock close to him. White hearts and two larger red hearts are shown against a pink background. Caption: "Gee, Somebody Cares." Anchor Hocking, 6¾", 1978. $8–$12

Snoopy and Woodstock compare their moves with the aerobic instruction sign. Another Woodstock is sitting on top of the sign. Caption: "We Superstars Stay in Shape." Anchor Hocking, 6¾", 1978.
$8–$12

Snoopy is wearing his tuxedo and top hat and is presenting flowers to Woodstock. Caption: "For You, On a Special Day!" Anchor Hocking, 6¾", 1978. $8–$12

Snoopy, in his dancing pose, caption: "Smile." Linus without his blanket, caption: "To Know Me Is to Love Me." Charlie Brown, caption: "I Need All the Friends I Can Get." (Picture seen): Lucy at her psychiatrist booth, caption: "For a Nickel I Can Cure Anything." Panels alternate colors of orange and blue. Anchor Hocking, 6¾", 1976. $12–$18

Silver

Snoopy is lying on top of a gold tone over silver heart-shaped vase. Box shows the same design. Leonard Silver, #9696, 4½", 1979.
$25–$35*

Snoopy, three-dimensional. He is clinging to the rim. Box shows same design. Leonard Silver, #9697, 8", 1979. $25–$35*

Playthings

When is a plaything not a toy or a game? While it is true that many of the items in this chapter could occupy a child's attention for relatively long periods of time, most of them are not quickly identifiable as a "toy" or a "game." For this reason we created a special chapter consisting of coloring and activity books, paint kits, minis, and puzzles, and we call it "Playthings."

Coloring books are one of the oldest categories of *Peanuts* collectibles, dating back to the late 1950s. They are still popular with today's generation of users as more and more come to the market every year. And they are also very much favored by *Peanuts* collectors.

The minis are interesting items. They are mostly useful adult products reduced in size to fit little children's hands to the point where they lose a good deal of their practicality. Yet they were very popular with the grade school set. Thus we have miniature tools, miniature phone books, miniature pencils, etc. Butterfly first came out with *Peanuts* minis in 1979. Since then the idea has been picked up and copied by countless other manufacturers featuring different characters.

One thing playthings have in common with toys and games is that adults don't normally buy them with the intention of actually playing with them. Certainly not the coloring books, minis, or six-piece puzzles. But, as with toys and games, they often find themselves buying two of everything—one for their kids to use and one for themselves to keep intact for their own collections.

COLORING AND ACTIVITY BOOKS

The Colorful World of Snoopy, Linus, Schroeder, Lucy, and Charlie Brown. Cover: in addition to the wording, this orange and green cover includes pictures of Linus with his blanket, Charlie Brown in baseball gear, Snoopy in his dancing pose, Schroeder at his piano, and Lucy skipping rope. Determined, 14″ × 19½″, early 1960s.

$30–$45

Parade Comics. . . . A Coloring Book Created by 33 Artists.'' Cover: Charlie Brown along with 13 other characters representing various comic strips. Inside: four pictures to color of the *Peanuts* characters. One picture features Snoopy and birds that are not Woodstock. Artcraft, mid 1960s.

$15–$20

Peanuts: A Book to Color. Cover: Snoopy and Charlie Brown on a skateboard. Saalfield, #4629, 1965.

$20–$30

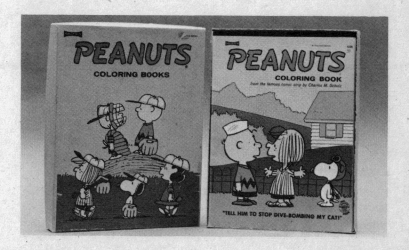

Peanuts Coloring Books. Boxed set of five. Box cover: Schroeder, the baseball catcher, confers with Charlie Brown on the baseball mound as players Peppermint Patty, Snoopy, and Lucy walk past them. (The following describes the five book covers.) Saalfield, #6546, late 1960s.

$35–$45*

Let's Play Ball. Schroeder and Charlie Brown in baseball gear are standing on the baseball mound. Peppermint Patty, Snoopy, and Lucy are walking by (repeat of box cover). #4574.

Life Is Difficult, Charlie Brown. Shows Charlie Brown's kite caught up in the trees with the string all tangled up. He thinks to himself, "Good Grief . . . !" Snoopy just stares with his ears sticking straight up. #4560.

"Tell Him to Stop Dive Bombing My Cat," Peppermint Patty tells Charlie Brown. Snoopy is standing behind Peppermint Patty. #4596.

Typically Lucy. Lucy with her big mouth tells Linus, "Why Shouldn't I Complain?" #4562.

Charlie Brown, Linus (sucking his thumb), Snoopy (lying on his house), and Lucy. #4564.

Peanuts Coloring Book. Cover: a puzzled Charlie Brown pushes a content Snoopy in a baby stroller. Caption on cover: "When I Asked Him to Go for a Walk, This Isn't Exactly What I Had in Mind." Saalfield, #5695, 1960s. $25–$30

Peanuts Coloring Book Featuring Snoopy. Cover: Lucy and Snoopy are ice skating. Caption: "Looking for a Partner, Sweetie?" Saalfield, #CO942, 1960s. $20–$25

Peanuts Coloring Book Featuring Violet. Cover: four panels featuring Lucy, Violet, and Snoopy. Violet and Lucy appear to be having an argument, using such words as "Nyaah!" and "Bleah!" Snoopy's thought balloon: "Girl Talk!" Saalfield, #9513, 1967. $35–$45

Peanuts "Great Pumpkin" Coloring Book. Cover: Linus and Snoopy in a pumpkin patch. Hallmark, #100HPF901-6, 1978. $12–$22

Peanuts Pictures to Color. Cover: Lucy and Charlie Brown are watching a bewildered Snoopy in a toy freight car as the train enters a tunnel that is too small to accommodate him. Saalfield, #5626, 1959. $25–$30

Peanuts Pictures to Color. Cover: Snoopy is snuggling up to Charlie Brown. In the background, smaller pictures of Lucy, Schroeder, Violet, and Patty are seen. Saalfield, #4523, 1959. $25–$30

Peanuts Projects. An activity book. The cover does not have the characters pictured on it. Inside are various projects for children to complete, including a maze puzzle, "Official Family Portrait" of the gang to paint, a play to enact with masks, as well as a sing-along with Schroeder. Determined, 1963. $20–$30

Peanuts Trace and Color. A five-book set. Cover of box: Charlie Brown looking at a ragged Snoopy. Caption: "Never Pick a Fight With a Hundred Pound Cat!" Saalfield, #6122, late 1960s.

$25–$35*

Snoopy and the Head Beagle. Snoopy is leaning against a croquet mallet.

Good Ol' Charlie Brown. Charlie Brown reads a letter as Snoopy looks on.

Peppermint Patty's Busy Day. Peppermint Patty holds a baseball bat and mitt as Snoopy, wearing a cap and glove, walks behind her.

Linus Looks at the World. Linus is standing while holding his famous blue blanket.

Lucy Does It Again. Lucy sits at her stand where she's selling "Goop 5¢." Charlie Brown digs into his pocket for money. He's going to actually try some of the stuff!

MINIS

Autograph Book. Cover: Charlie Brown and Lucy, with Woodstock nearby, wave at a strutting Snoopy. Caption: "Autographs." Butterfly, #119 0717, 1980. $1.50–$2

Paperweight, ceramic. Snoopy is sitting on a blue base typing. Caption: "Love Letters." Includes a pencil. Butterfly, #0200 0911, 2″ × 2¾″, 1980. $3–$4*

Pencil cup, ceramic. Snoopy, hugging a poorly defined Woodstock, sits next to a red barrel. The barrel holds miniature pencils and is captioned "Love." Butterfly, #119 0717, 1¾″ × 2″, 1980 (see photo on previous page, right). $3–$4*

School Bus Pencil Case. Miniature plastic bus with Snoopy, Sally, Charlie Brown, Peppermint Patty, and Lucy. Pencils inside. Pencil sharpener in rear. Butterfly, #0744, 1981. $2.50–$3.50

Message Board (hard plastic). Message pad and pencil are attached to a house-shaped board with Snoopy's name and picture at top. Woodstock is nearby. A Woodstock tassel is attached for use in hanging on wall. Butterfly, #99 0730, 1980. $1.50–$2

Snoopy's Mini Mailbox. A clear plastic miniature mailbox with Snoopy on one side and three Woodstocks on the other. Inside is a miniature notebook, pencil, stationery, and envelopes. Butterfly, #200 0817-2, 1981. $3.50–$4

Snoopy Tiny Tools tool case (blue or red). Captioned "Snoopy" with five miniature tools in a blister pack. Butterfly, #175 7809-1, 1981.
$2–$3*

Mini Binder. Miniature clip board, plastic. Snoopy and Woodstock at the typewriter appear on the clasp. Linus and Sally depicted on the pad. Butterfly, #119 0713, 1979.
$1.50–$2

Snoopy Dress Up Set (similar to regular-sized Colorforms). Cover: Snoopy on a ladder next to a big picture of Snoopy wearing a cowboy hat. Butterfly, #169 0840-2, 1982.
$3–$4*

Snoopy Mini Index. Cover: Snoopy on the phone which is connected to Woodstock's nest. For keeping phone numbers. Hard plastic. Butterfly, #149 1745, 1980.
$2–$3

PAINT KITS

Snoopy Big Set. This is a paint-by-number set. Box cover: a collage of several scenes on one canvas featuring Snoopy, Linus, Lucy, Woodstock, and Charlie Brown. Craft House, 12″ × 16″, early 1980s.
$12–$20*

Snoopy's Fast-Dry Paint-by-Number on Black Velvet. Titled: "Lunch for Two." Box cover: Sally sits on a bench. Linus is holding his lunch. Craft House/Determined, #8573, early 1980s. $5–$12*

Snoopy Wood Painting. Snoopy, Charlie Brown, and Linus are in a baseball scene. Craft House/Determined, #6074, early 1980s.

$8–$14*

Snoopy's Wood Painting Christmas Ornaments. Box cover: 20 ornaments to paint by number are shown, all using the *Peanuts* characters in one pose or another. Craft House, #8070, early 1980s.

$20–$30*

PUZZLES

Schroeder, Charlie Brown, Snoopy, and Lucy are on a baseball mound. They're all dressed in baseball outfits. Milton Bradley, #4383-3, 1973. $10–$20*

Eight-panel cartoon strip. Lucy jumping rope turned by Linus and Charlie Brown. Caption: "Peanuts." 1000 pieces. Determined, #711-2, 24″ × 24″, 1971. $20–$30*

Four complete cartoon strips. Features the characters Lucy, Schroeder, Snoopy, Linus, and Charlie Brown. Arranged so that each grouping faces the outside. 1000 pieces. Determined, #711-3, 24″ × 24″, 1971. $20–$30*

Love Is. Four scenes, each with a different "Love Is" theme and each occupying one quarter of the puzzle. Features Charlie Brown and Snoopy ("Love Is Having Someone to Lean On"), Linus and Sally ("Love Is Tickling"), Shermy and Patty ("Love Is Walking Hand-in-Hand"), and Schroeder and Lucy ("Love Is Mussing Up Someone's Hair"). 1000 pieces. Determined, #711-4, 24″ × 24″, 1971.
$25–$35*

Snoopy, wearing a baseball hat and leaning on his bat. Six pieces. Playskool, #230-27 "Superstar," 1979. $8–$12*

A troubled Charlie Brown goes to visit Lucy at her psychiatrist booth. Lucy says to Chuck, "For a Nickel I Can Cure Anything." Playskool, #230-19, 1979. $8–$15*

Toys and Games

Toys and games. Games and toys. The very words evoke memories of our own childhood and, for we older collectors, the years our children were growing up.

Toys and games were meant to be ripped out of the box, enjoyed, shared, and used many, many times, over and over again. Right? Wrong, if you are a collector. It is the irony of collecting that the more a toy or game has been used and enjoyed, the less monetary value it has. This is particularly true of games, so much so that games out of the box will not even be spoken of in this section. Some toys, however, like the Talking Bus and the die-cast toys, will retain a good deal of their value even out of the box.

The operative phrase here is "mint in the box" (MIB). Game and toy boxes must be in good to mint condition and hopefully sealed. In some cases, if a toy's box is not sealed the value is diminished.

If you must consider the purchase of a toy or game out of the box, it behooves you to at least assure yourself that no parts are missing, that all movable parts are working properly, and that the seller guarantees that battery-operated toys will function as intended when the battery is inserted. (Some collectors bring batteries on their hunts.) You should also, in most cases where the toy or game is out of the box, pay a small fraction of the prices listed in this guide.

Metal toys are greatly in demand, especially toys by Chein, and they retain a good deal of their value even out of the box. An example of this is the Talking Bus. The speaking mechanism is controlled by a rubber band which is almost impossible to reach and replace without irrevocably damaging the toy. The Talking Bus is now about 25 years old. Over that length of time the rubber band is sure to become stretched out and useless. Consequently, a Talking Bus in mint condition hardly exists and collectors more and more are overlooking condition in order to own one.

The tools required to make die-cast or plastic toys are big and heavy. Over the years a large number of them have been lost, believe it or not, or deliberately destroyed because there was no room to store them. Therefore, certain toys can never be recreated exactly. And the great expense of designing new tools will preclude the making of replicas in the future. On the other hand, tools that have not been lost or destroyed can easily be put back into production. It is therefore well within the realm of possibility that large quantities of certain die-cast items can reappear in the future.

A list of Aviva tools which are gone forever would be quite lengthy. Some of the more noteworthy include the Snoopy mini die-cast Family Car (#2028); the larger Family Car in the 700 series; the Snoopy Gyro Cycle (#70440); two Formula-1 Racing Cars (#950), one with Snoopy and one with Woodstock; the Climbing String Woodstock (#667); the Snoopy Battery-Operated Speedway (#999); the Snoopy Express Station Train Set (#988); and Snoopy the Critic (#222). The Critic is extremely rare—less than 1000 were produced—and should be the "find for the future."

It is interesting to note that wooden toys, which preceded the plastic variety, were of excellent workmanship and are prized by many collectors. Notable among these are the Wooden Train (Aviva, #911) and the Wooden Windup Train Set (Aviva, #922).

MIB (Mint In Box): Item in unopened box, box in excellent condition.

Mint Condition: Superior quality, box missing.

Good Condition: All parts are included. Item and/or box shows limited wear and tear.

Poor Condition: Major wear and tear. Parts may be missing.

ACTION

Snoopy Action Toy Starring Snoopy. Snoopy is wearing a football helmet and his foot is ready in a kicking position. Depress his helmet and he kicks the football placed on the base. Plastic. Aviva, #200, 1977. $15–$25*

Snoopy Action Toy Starring Charlie Brown. Charlie Brown is wearing a baseball cap and holding a bat. A ball is attached to a spring and when you depress Chuck's hat, it activates his hand and he hits the ball. Plastic. Aviva, #200, 1977. $20–$30*

Snoopy Action Toy Starring Snoopy. Snoopy has on a helmet and in his hand he is holding a hockey stick. On the base is a puck. When you depress Snoopy's helmet, it activates his hand and he hits the puck. Plastic. Aviva, #200, 1977. $15–$25*

Good Grief Glider. An airplane with Snoopy as the Flying Ace is propelled off a powerful spring loader launcher. Flies up to 20 feet. For indoor or outdoor use. The box shows some children operating the glider. Plastic. Child Guidance, #1775, late 1970s. $30–$45*

Peanuts Push Puppets. A slight depression at the base will send these three-dimensional characters wiggling. Plastic. Ideal, #5350-4, 1977.

Snoopy the sheriff. $20–$30

Lucy the nurse wearing a white uniform. $25–$35

Joe Cool Snoopy wearing orange turtleneck and brown shades.
$15–$20

Snoopy the World War I Flying Ace. $20–$25

Charlie Brown the baseball manager. $25–$35

Snoopy the magician dressed in black tuxedo and top hat.
$25–$35

Peanuts Top. The faces of Snoopy, Charlie Brown, Lucy, and Linus appear on a brightly colored background. When you push the top in and then pull up, the top will begin to spin and pick up speed. Metal. Chein, #263, late 1960s. $65–$85*

Peanuts Top. Peppermint Patty, Linus sitting with his blanket, Charlie Brown talking to Snoopy, and Schroeder at his piano with Lucy leaning on it are pictured against a white background with orange and blue circle motif. Metal. Chein, late 1960s. $50–$80*

Peanuts Skediddler Club House Set with Charlie Brown, Lucy, and Snoopy. The three skediddlers are packed together in a box with a club house design. Hold the back plastic attachment and push to see the skediddlers walk. They each wear the same clothing as described on the individual skediddlers listed later in this chapter. Rubber. Mattel, #3803, 1970. $45–$125*

Skediddlers. Rubber. By pushing the plastic wheel attachment, you can make the skediddlers walk. Mattel, 1969.

Snoopy as the Flying Ace. He's wearing brown helmet, green plastic goggles, and a red scarf. #3630. $15–$40*

Lucy. #3631. Lucy wears a dark blue dress with a white lace collar. Her shoes and socks are painted. $15–$40*

Charlie Brown. #3632. Charlie wears a yellow shirt with black zigzag and black pants. His shoes and socks are painted. $15–$40*

Linus. #3634. A red and white striped shirt, dark blue pants, along with painted shoes and socks, complete his attire. He holds a light blue blanket. $25–$50*

Snoopy and Charlie Brown Copter. Place Snoopy or Charlie Brown in a slot on top of Snoopy's doghouse, pull the cord, and watch the rotor blades on top of their heads twirl as they are launched into the air (one at a time). Plastic. Aviva/Hasbro, #600, 1979. $35–$45*

Snoopy Deep Diver Submarine. The trigger mechanism on the squeeze control makes it dive and surface. It comes with a floating Woodstock. Plastic. Knickerbocker, #0553, early 1980s. $35–$45*

Snoopy Gravity Raceway. Lift the starting gate and Snoopy, Woodstock, Charlie Brown, and Lucy race down a double-track raceway. The first car to reach the bottom wins. Plastic. Aviva, #990, 1977.

$45–$55*

Snoopy Gyro Cycle. Features Snoopy driving his motorcycle. Charlie Brown is sitting in the side car and Woodstock is sitting next to him. It has a friction motor and balance friction action. See-through box. Plastic. Hasbro/Aviva, #70440, 1982. $30–$45*

Snoopy High Wire Act (Snap Tite kit). Snoopy, with moving legs, pedals his unicycle on a high wire carrying Woodstock, who is on a trapeze that is attached to the unicycle wheel. A player is holding the rope Snoopy is on and activating him across to his house. Monogram/Mattel, #6661, 1973. $30–$40*

Snoopy Skediddler and His Sopwith Camel. Open the black carrying case and find Snoopy as the Flying Ace in his biplane. They pop up and you can walk Snoopy by pushing the back attachment. The outside cover of the toy shows Snoopy yelling "Curse You Red Baron!" Carrying case came in other colors. Mattel, #4954, 1969.

$75–$150*

Snoopy's Stunt Spectacular. Snoopy is propelled on a cycle that can break apart upon crashing and then can easily be reassembled. The cover of the box illustrates how the toy works by showing a young boy playing with it. Plastic. Child Guidance, #1750, 1978.

$60–$70*

Woodstock Climbing String Action. Gently pull the string and Woodstock climbs up and down on the string. At the same time, his wings move and a chirping sound is heard. Plastic. Aviva/Hasbro, #667, 1977.

$25–$35*

ACTIVITY

Pegs Accessory Pack. Colorful pictures that light up and glow. Contains 24 Lite Brite pictures and 24 colored pegs, using the *Peanuts* characters. (Can only be used in conjunction with Hasbro's "Lite Brite Toy.") Hasbro, #5478, 1984. $15–$20*

Picture Maker. Features *Peanuts* plastic stencils which help the user create pictures and scenes of Charlie Brown, Linus, Lucy, and Snoopy. The box cover shows two children using the toy and the pictures you can create. Mattel, #4153 (paper box), 1971.

$30–$38*

Super Cartoon Maker. Features Snoopy and his *Peanuts* pals. It contains the necessary materials, including cast iron molds to form five characters with 14 different poses. The box cover depicts the characters, Snoopy, Charlie Brown, Linus, Lucy, and a bird (not Woodstock), as you would make them by using Plastigoop, and what you can use the finished product for. Mattel, #4696, 1970. $90–$125*

Snoopy Color 'N' Recolor. It contains the necessary materials to decorate mugs, bowls, and placemats. The box cover shows some children using the materials to create. Avalon, #742, 1980. $25–$35*

Snoopy Sign Mobile. Material needed to make Snoopy and his friends are included. The box cover shows the sign mobile when it is put together. A little girl is shown using a stencil, crayon, and preprinted paper that are part of the supplies. Avalon, #262, late 1970s. $50–$70*

BALANCE

Balance Bar, Woodstock, Charlie Brown, and Snoopy. This toy comes complete with stand, balance bar, swings, and *Peanuts* characters. (Several different combinations of three *Peanuts* characters were manufactured in blister pack and window box.) Blister pack shown here. High impact plastic. Aviva, #150, 1979. $18–$25*

Balance Bar, Lucy, Snoopy, and Charlie Brown. This toy comes complete with stand, balance bar, swings, and *Peanuts* characters. (Several different combinations of three *Peanuts* characters were manufactured in blister pack and window box.) Window box is shown. High impact plastic. Aviva, #155, 1979. $20–$30*

Balance Toy, Snoopy and Woodstock on Doghouse. This toy is weighted and easily balanced. Aviva, #555 blister packed, #560 boxed, 1980. $20–$30*

Balance Toy, Snoopy and Woodstock Scouting. This toy is weighted and easily balanced. Aviva, #555 blister packed, #560 boxed, 1979.
$25–$35*

BATTERY OPERATED

Chirping Woodstock. With electronic sound. Turn on the button and you get a tune. When Woodstock's tail is pushed up, down, to the right or to the left you get four different bird calls. Plastic. Aviva, #477, 1977. $10–$30*

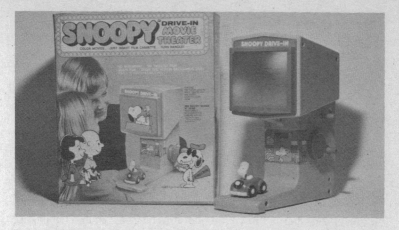

Drive-In Movie Theater. Decal below the screen shows Woodstock serving refreshments. Caption on drive-in: "Snoopy Drive-In." Snoopy is sitting in his red convertible, leaning all the way back to see the screen. Plastic. Just insert the cassette, turn the handle, and view the color movies. (Cassettes may also be used with Snoopy hand-held movie viewer.) Kenner, #39570, 1975. $95–$125*

Electronic Snoopy Playmate. You can play the game "Snoopy Says" three ways. By hitting different objects you can play seven popular songs. Or, play and record your own music and then use the playback feature. On the front, Snoopy appears as a parade leader. He is joined by Woodstock and surrounded by three colored lights. Each object is used for a purpose. Plastic. Romper Room/Hasbro, #830, 1980. $90–$120*

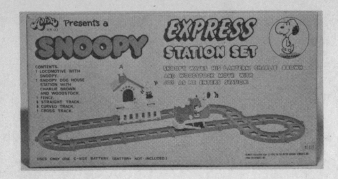

Express Station Set. Snoopy, waving a lantern, rides a locomotive. As the locomotive passes the "doghouse station," Woodstock (in chimney) and Charlie Brown (on platform) move as locomotive passes the station. Plastic. Aviva, #988, 1977. $85–$110*

Peanuts Talking Bus. Snoopy, as the driver, bunnies, pre-Woodstock birds, Linus, Schroeder, Pigpen, Frieda, Charlie Brown, and Lucy are seen at the windows. Five and Sally are seen through the back window. Caption on both sides of bus: "Happiness Is an Annual Outing." When a button on top is depressed, the characters sing and speak. Metal. J. Chein & Co., #261, 1967. $250–$275*

Rowing Snoopy. Snoopy is in a blue boat using red oars and Woodstock is at the helm. Snoopy can row to the right, to the left or straight ahead. Plastic. Mattel, #3478, 1981. $25–$35*

Rowing Snoopy. Snoopy is in a blue boat using red oars and Woodstock is at the helm. Snoopy can row to the right, to the left or straight ahead. (This is the original.) Plastic. Concept 2000, #107, late 1970s. $35–$45*

Swimming Snoopy. Snoopy on his back makes himself at home in the water. The turning of his ears, activated by the battery, propels him. Plastic. Concept 2000, #106, late 1970s. $20–$40*

Schroeder's Piano. On the top of the blue piano sit removable rubber figures of Snoopy, Lucy, Charlie Brown, Peppermint Patty, Schroeder, and Linus, who pop up as the piano is played. Plastic. Child Guidance, #1701, mid 1970s. $75–$85*

An asterisk (*) next to a price indicates that the item comes with its original box in excellent condition. If no asterisk is shown, there is no box or the box adds little significant value. Shipping boxes (no graphics) are of no value.

———————

A copyright date indicates the year the character first appeared in a particular incarnation, *not* the year the product first came out.

Snoopy the Critic. Snoopy and Woodstock in his nest sit on top of Snoopy's house. Ask a friend to sing or tell a funny story into the microphone. Push a button on the microphone and Snoopy claps away and Woodstock jumps up and down. Plastic. Aviva, #222, 1977. $100-$150*

Snoopy Family Car. Snoopy is driving and Lucy sits with him. Peppermint Patty and Charlie Brown sit in the rear. Woodstock is the head ornament. When the car is in motion, the lights blink on and off. If it should bump into a wall, it turns around and goes the other way. Often called the "mystery car." Plastic. Aviva, #2700, 1978. $25-$50*

Snoopy & His Flyin' Doghouse. By an extended wire, Charlie Brown keeps Snoopy on his doghouse in the air. With a hand lever you can sway and loop and knock down the Red Baron who is positioned on the ground. Mattel, #8263, 1974. $65-$85*

Woodstock Formula-1 Racing Car. Woodstock races in his flashy orange, purple, yellow, and white car with authentic racing sound and steerable front wheels. Plastic. Aviva, #950, 11½″, 1978.

$55–$80*

Snoopy Formula-1 Racing Car. Snoopy races in his flashy orange, purple, yellow, and white car with authentic racing sound and steerable front wheels. Plastic. Aviva, #950, 11½″, 1978.   *$55–$80**

Snoopy Speedway. The speedway comes with a track holding tower, starting sign, four race cars, starting gate, and tracks. The tracks are set up like a cyclone ride. You start the cars at the top. The one that returns to the starting gate first wins. Plastic. Aviva, #999, 1977.

$80–$100*

Snoopy is Joe Cool (Snap Tite kit). Snoopy wears white and blue surf shorts as well as shades. As he stands on his surfboard, he rides the ocean waves and can even spin around on the board. Monogram/Mattel, #7502, 1971. $45–$60*

Snoopy-Matic Instant Load Camera. Snoopy is on his tummy hanging off his doghouse. His house is the camera. Uses 110 film. Helm Toy Corp., #975, late 1970s. $75–$100*

Snoopy Racing Car Stickshifter. Snoopy sits in the driver's seat as the Flying Ace. Woodstock in his nest sits on the front of this yellow racer with pink and lavender trim. Caption: "Snoopy" where Snoopy sits and "Woodstock" where Woodstock sits. You control the speed by using a hand lever which is next to the ramp. He then takes off from the ramp. Aviva, #2500, 1978. $75–$125*

Snoopy Radio Controlled Doghouse (with remote control). Snoopy is lying on his house, captioned "Snoopy." By depressing Woodstock's tail, you control the motions of the house. Plastic. Aviva, #988, 1980. $60–$75*

Snoopy Radio Controlled Fire Engine (with Woodstock transmitter). Snoopy is wearing a fireman's hat. Woodstock is standing nearby. Charlie Brown and Lucy, wearing firemen's hats, are sitting in the back near the movable white ladder. You control the fire engine by depressing Woodstock's tail. Plastic. Aviva, #988 R/C, 1980.
$65–$85*

Snoopy Slot Car Racing Set. Hand units control Charlie Brown and Snoopy as they compete along a green plastic race course. Aviva, #XL500, 1977. $85–$100*

Snoopy Snippers. These scissors are in the form of Snoopy lying on his tummy. The blades are inside his mouth. Plastic. Mattel, #7410, 1975. $35–$45*

MIB (Mint In Box): Item in unopened box, box in excellent condition.

Mint Condition: Superior quality, box missing.

Good Condition: All parts are included. Item and/or box shows limited wear and tear.

Poor Condition: Major wear and tear. Parts may be missing.

Snoopy and His Bugatti Race Car (Snap Tite Model Kit). Snoopy, with a head that turns, sits in his red Bugatti captioned "Snoopy." The car also has a picture of him along with a "#4." A white display base to hold the Bugatti when not in use is captioned "Snoopy and His Bugatti." Monogram/Mattel, #6894, 1971. $45-$60*

Snoopy and His Motorcycle (with Woodstock in the sidecar). This is a Snap Tite Model Kit. It has motorized wheels and a steerable front wheel. Uses two AA batteries. Box top shows Snoopy in the motorcycle with Woodstock in the sidecar captioned "Snoopy and His Motorcycle." Capable of racing around the room. Monogram/Mattel, #5902, 1971. $45-$60*

Snoopy and His Sopwith Camel (Snap Tite Model Kit). Top of the box shows the assembled Sopwith. Inside is a replica of the front of Snoopy's house, which is used as a stand for the plane. If you give the propellors a flip, they will spin. The side of the plane is captioned "Snoopy" and there are stick-on insignias. Thought balloons are included and read "Curse You Red Baron!" and "Gotcha!" Monogram/Mattel, #6779, 1971. $40-$55*

Snoopy Toothbrush. Snoopy, as the unit that holds the toothbrush, is lying on the top of his house. You remove him and place one of the two brushes included into the top of Snoopy's head. Plastic. Kenner, #30301, 1972. $35–$45*

Snoopy Train Set. Schroeder is driving the locomotive captioned "Snoopy Express." Behind the blue locomotive is Charlie Brown in a coal tender (which is meant to look like a baseball mound). It is captioned "Charlie Brown." Snoopy's doghouse car follows with Snoopy lying on top. It is captioned "Snoopy." Woodstock is in his tree car captioned "Woodstock." To complete the set, railroad signs, doghouse ticket booth, blue tracks, and a green tunnel are included. Aviva, #3000, 1977. $75–$95*

Snoopy's Beagle Bugle. Snoopy with a horn and Woodstock with a drum, dressed as scouts, sit on top of the green bugle. The decal on the side of the bugle pictures Snoopy and Woodstock as scouts joined by Charlie Brown with a banner captioned "Troop 528." When you depress the mouthpiece, a miniature phonograph inside plays a rousing bugle call. Plastic. Child Guidance, #1730, late 1970s.

$45–$75*

Snoopy's Dream Machine. Smaller version of Snoopy on his dog-house chasing the Red Baron on his Fokker, but without blinking lights. Laminated cardboard. DCS, #417-M, 1980. $50–$70*

Snoopy's Dream Machine. Fanciful reproduction of Snoopy on his yellow house chasing the Red Baron in his Fokker. Comes complete with blinking lights. Needs assembling. Laminated cardboard. DCS, 1979. $60–$110*

Snoopy's 'Lectric Comb & Brush. Snoopy lies in a blue boat that holds on one side a brush and on the other a comb. When the comb or brush is inserted into Snoopy's head, they vibrate. Box cover: two children using the item. Plastic. Kenner, #30900, 1975. $40–$50*

Snoopy's Pencil Sharpener. Snoopy is at the typewriter on the roof of his house. Directly behind him is the pencil sharpener. The entire item stands on a green base that holds pencils. Box cover: Lucy is using the sharpener and Charlie Brown is waiting his turn. Plastic. Kenner, #3550, 1974. $35–$45*

Table Top Snoopy (Game and Watch). The general idea of the game: Schroeder is playing his piano; the notes fly through the air to where Woodstock is sleeping; you operate Snoopy right and left to strike down the notes with his hammer, so Woodstock can sleep. Nintendo, #SM-73, early 1980s. $75–$85*

COSTUMES AND PROPS

Megaphone. Caption: "Head Beagle." Pictured: Snoopy as a director, Lucy, and Charlie Brown. Written beneath their pictures: "Stars of the Movie *A Boy Named Charlie Brown*." This came in a variety of colors. Metal with plastic mouthpiece. J. Chein & Co., 1970.

$10–$20

Peanuts Costume. This one will make the child look like Charlie Brown at Halloween time. Box cover caption: "*Peanuts Costume*." Pictures of Lucy, Charlie Brown, Sally, Snoopy, Schroeder, Peppermint Patty, and Linus appear on the box. Determined, #6300, early 1970s.

$15–$30*

Snoopy on Parade. Drum Majorette and Cheerleader. Consists of a paper megaphone, two fluffy pompoms, Snoopy baton, and a Snoopy whistle. The box front depicts Snoopy leading the gang, Linus with a tuba, Lucy with pompoms, Charlie Brown with cymbals, and Woodstock with a whistle. See-through box. Synergistics, #PMS-15, 1982.

$35–$45*

EDUCATIONAL

Push and Play With the Peanuts Gang. The gang includes Charlie Brown, Lucy, Linus, Peppermint Patty, and Snoopy in their own playhouse. If the proper wagon holder is pushed, the character's door is opened and he or she can come out and play in wagons that can be hitched up together. Snoopy in his doghouse and the gang in their wagons can ride down the ramp. Side not seen is window boxed. Brightly colored. Plastic. Rubber characters. Child Guidance, #1700, late 1970s. $40–$55*

See 'N Say Snoopy Says. Select the picture by turning Snoopy's hand toward it and you can hear the matching phrase. (Linus says "Happiness Is a Thumb and Blanket.") This helps build picture and word relationships. The pictures are of the gang, consisting of Sally and Snoopy, Frieda, Snoopy, Pigpen, Linus, Peppermint Patty, Snoopy, Charlie Brown, Violet, Schroeder, and Lucy. Mattel, #4864, 1969. $75–$90*

Snoopy's Shape Register. This brightly colored toy has eight geometric fittings. The child coordinates the eight color-coded shapes with the fittings. The keys each have a shape and color. If the shape fits the fitting and a coordinated key is pushed, the shape disappears. Pull the Snoopy handle, a bell rings, the drawer opens, and the shapes reappear. Box: shows a little girl playing with the toy. Plastic. Gabriel/Child Guidance, #51740, 1980. $35–$45*

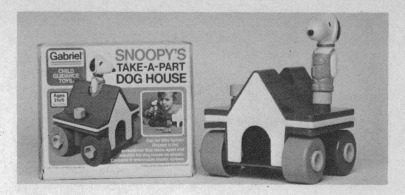

Snoopy's Take-a-Part Doghouse. Snoopy is the screwdriver that takes apart and rebuilds the doghouse, which is on wheels. Consists of six removable plastic screws. Box: shows toy that is inside and a little child taking it apart. Very colorful. Plastic. Gabriel/Child Guidance, #51705, 1980. $25–$30*

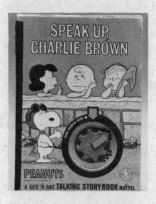

Speak Up, Charlie Brown. This is a talking storybook. If you pull the string you can read and hear at the same time. Cover: Lucy, Charlie Brown, and Linus leaning on a brick wall. In front of the wall stands Snoopy as an English aviator. Hard cardboard. Vinyl-type pages. Mattel, #4812, 1971. $90–$110*

Stack-Up Snoopy. This consists of six big, durable, stay-together pieces. When you put Scoutmaster Snoopy together, you can play with him as a doll. His head, belly, and scarf spin. His hat and feet lock onto a center post. Side not shown is window boxed. Sides show how Snoopy is to be put together and a child doing it. Plastic. Romper Room/Hasbro, #818, 5½″ × 5½″ × 9½″, 1980.

$25–$30*

Tell Time Clock, Snoopy. This clock runs up to eight hours. A child can take it apart and put it together (ask your child if you can't do it). Window boxed. Snoopy is in the center of the clock and his hands hold red arrows to point to the numbers. The bells on top are decorative. Plastic. Concept 2000, #171, early 1980s. $20–$30*

Tell Time Clock, Charlie Brown. This clock runs up to eight hours. A child can take it apart and put it together. Window boxed. Charlie Brown is in the center of the clock. The blue arrows in his hands point to the numbers. The bells on top are decorative. Plastic. Concept 2000, #172, early 1980s. $25–$35*

Tell Time Clock, Woodstock. This clock runs up to eight hours A child can take it apart and put it together. Window boxed. Woodstock is in the center and the flower on a stem points to the numbers. The bells on top are decorative. Plastic. Concept 2000, #173, early 1980s. $25–$30*

GAMES

Can You Catch It, Charlie Brown? The player sends a big plastic ball into the field by using the handle with a spring action. The bell rings while the ball is in the field to alert the players. The big gloves they are wearing wait for the ball. If it lands in a glove, it is caught. Box cover: two children are playing the game. Ideal, #8282-6, 1976.

$80–$100*

Charlie Brown's All-Stars. This game has a baseball theme and the player must get the most runs to win. Box cover: Schroeder is wearing his catcher's mask, Snoopy just hit a ball, Charlie Brown, Pigpen, and Lucy are watching it fly. Woodstock is running out of the way. Parker Brothers, #410, 1974.

$20–$30*

Good Ol' Charlie Brown. The object is for a player to collect the most picture cards of his character (which is chosen by each player at the start of the game). Box cover: shows Charlie Brown standing and in the background Woodstock is playing hockey in a birdbath. Milton Bradley, #4139, 1972.

$25–$35*

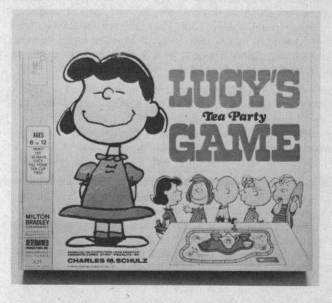

Lucy's Tea Party Game. Players pick their favorite *Peanuts* character and they are that character for the game. Lucy travels on the vinyl game sheet and is controlled by the throwing of dice. She allows the players who have chosen characters Sally, Peppermint Patty, Linus, or Charlie Brown to add cubes of sugar, spoons, and squirts of tea (water) to their teacup. The teapot stays in the center of the board and holds the water. First player to fill his cup wins. Box cover: shows the board set up and the characters Charlie Brown, Peppermint Patty, Sally, Lucy, and Linus. Milton Bradley, #4129, 1972.

$30–$40*

Peanuts, The Game of Charlie Brown and His Pals. The first player to form a complete sequence of cards numbered 1, 2, 3, 4, and 5 or any four of these numbers, plus the *Peanuts* card, is the winner. Cover of box: Charlie Brown, Violet, Patty, Schroeder, Lucy, Pigpen, Shermy, and Linus chasing Snoopy, who is running with a ball in his mouth. Selchow & Richter, #86, late 1960s. $20–$30*

Snoopy Card Game. The players must try to pass the Ha Ha card to the other players to keep them from getting Friend cards. If they get a Ha Ha, they must go back on the board. The players keep going until one arrives at "Finish," and that player wins. Box cover: Snoopy, wearing a visor, is holding cards. He and Woodstock are on the roof of his house. Milton Bradley, #4425, 1975. $12–$20*

Snoopy Come Home. A little girl named Lila owned Snoopy before Charlie Brown. She is now sick and in the hospital. Snoopy and Woodstock set out to see her. They stay with her until she recovers. At Lila's request, he goes home with her and sees a sign posted in her apartment building that no dogs are allowed. And a cat lives next door. Now the game starts. The gang sets out to find him. Milton Bradley, #4303, 1975. $12–$20*

Snoopy & The Red Baron. One plays the Red Baron and the other plays Snoopy. The Red Baron gets ten marbles and during his turn must get them into Snoopy's house without Snoopy catching him. This game is played in rounds. Then the players switch places and now the new Red Baron attempts to do the same. Score is kept until one player gets ten points. Box cover: Snoopy sitting on his house as an angry Flying Ace. Lucy, Linus, and Charlie Brown, who is yelling "Good Grief, I Goofed!," are all standing around. Milton Bradley, #4067, 1970. $10–$20*

Snoopy Snack Attack. Snoopy is in his house and a bowl of plastic-shaped bones are in front of his door. The players must pick out the bones one at a time without the door popping open. If it does and Snoopy appears, the player lost. Box cover: two girls are playing the game. Gabriel, #70345, 1980. $20–$30*

Snoopy's Doghouse Game. A plastic doghouse is completely built in the course of playing the game. Box cover: it shows all the pieces of the house apart and together. Snoopy is walking toward the house with a hammer. Milton Bradley, #4704, 1977. $20–$30*

Snoopy's Pound-a-Ball. A *Peanuts* version of a vertical pinball machine. When you pound the ball and it goes in any of the proper slots, the character in that space moves up to the tree house. When you get them all up, you win. Plastic. Gabriel/Child Guidance, #51702, 1980. $60–$70*

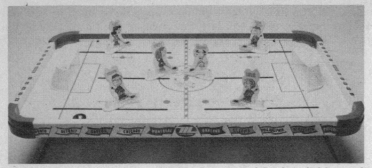

Tabletop Hockey. On this red and white, metal hockey field, are the players Schroeder, Peppermint Patty, Lucy, Linus, Snoopy, and Charlie Brown. Two players are needed to control the teams and score points for their side. Box cover: Snoopy, Charlie Brown, and Lucy on ice skates and with hockey sticks in their hands. Two children are playing the game. Box captioned "Snoopy and His Pals Play Hockey." Munro Games/Determined, 1972. $95–$125*

Tell Us a Riddle, Snoopy. On one side of the board is a series of questions in a circle, and on the other are the answers. A hard cardboard Snoopy, a wand in his hand and a magnet as his base, stands in the center of the questions. After turning and pointing to a question that is asked by either Lucy, Woodstock, Charlie Brown or Linus, he is put on the side with the answers. He turns and picks out the correct one. Box cover: Snoopy on the magnet base holds the wand and points to the sign in Linus's hand. They are surrounded by Lucy, Woodstock, and Charlie Brown. Colorforms, #2397, 1974.

$30–$40*

HOBBIES

Coins of the President. This collector book has spaces for coins. The cover depicts Snoopy carrying an American flag. Jerry Briskin Enterprises, 1970s. $15–$20

Peanuts Sculpt-Sure, Charlie Brown. After the form is pressed together, it is filled with Stay-Soft clay. Box: a picture of a finished Charlie Brown with baseball hat and glove; also, a child making one. Mattel, #8956, 12″, 1972. $50–$65*

Peanuts Sculpt-Sure, Snoopy. After the form is pressed together, it is filled with Stay-Soft clay. Box: a picture of a finished Snoopy as the Flying Ace. A child is seen working on one. Mattel, #8957, 10½″, 1972. $50–$65*

Snoopy Astronaut Commemorative Coin. This was released to commemorate the Apollo flight in 1969. The package shows Snoopy as an astronaut, bubble on his head and flight bag. This silver-toned coin depicts Snoopy as an astronaut on one side and Snoopy as an astronaut on his doghouse on the reverse side. Determined, #311, 1969. $25–$40*

Snoopy's Penny Coin Collection Book. This collector book has spaces for coins. The cover depicts Snoopy as the Flying Ace. Jerry Briskin Enterprises, 1970s. $15–$20

INFLATABLES

Beach ball. Features Snoopy in his dancing pose. Caption: "This Is the Life!" Ideal, #5618-4, 24", 1976. $10–$20*

Charlie Brown punching bag. Caption: "I Need All the Friends I Can Get." Determined, early 1970s. $30–$45*

Joe Cool punching bag. His shirt is captioned "Joe Cool." "Snoopy" is captioned at the base. Ideal, #5530–1, 36", 1976. $20–$25*

Peanuts Party Play Chair. Size-wise it is made for a preschooler. The chair is red and the backrest is a yellow and white check. It is decorated with all the *Peanuts* gang. Ideal, #5385-0, 1977. $30–$40*

Woodstock (with crazy spring and squeaker). He bounces about as he hangs from the spring and so Ideal gave him the name of "Fluttering Woodstock" in its advertisements. Ideal, #5315-0, 15″, 1977.

$10–$30*

INSTRUMENTS/MUSIC

Peanuts Kindergarten Rhythm Set. Box cover: Lucy with 6″ tambourine, Snoopy with cymbals, Charlie Brown with 9″ drum and beater, and Woodstock with triangle and striker. These are the percussion instruments that are inside the box. Metal. J. Chein & Co., #327, 1972.

$95–$130*

Peanuts Drum. Design on drum features Lucy with baton, Charlie Brown playing trombone, Snoopy walking (on all fours), Schroeder playing his piano, and Pigpen holding an American flag and pulling Schroeder in a wagon. Sally is playing the trumpet and Linus is hitting the bass drum, which is captioned ''*Peanuts* Marching Band and Good Grief Society.'' Metal. A. Chein Industries Co., #1713, 1974.

$65-$85*

Peanuts Parade Drum. Design features Charlie Brown, Snoopy, Lucy, Linus, Schroeder, Sally, Frieda, and Pigpen sitting in directors' chairs. Drumsticks included. Metal. J. Chein & Co., #1798, 1969.

$80-$125*

Piano. Pictured on top is Schroeder at the piano, Lucy leaning on it, Snoopy standing on it playing a fiddle, and Linus with his blanket. Wood. Ely, late 1960s.

$90-$150*

Snoopy's Harp. Nothing on the harp identifies it with any *Peanuts* characters. However, since Snoopy played the harp in the motion picture *A Boy Named Charlie Brown*, the box, depicting Snoopy playing the harp, is attractive to the collector. Trophy Music Co., 1969-1970.

$10-$15*

Snoopy in the Music Box. Music plays as you turn the handle and stops when Snoopy pops out. Picture on front of the metal box shows Snoopy with a concertina. A bird (not Woodstock) is holding the notes for Snoopy to follow. Mattel, #4747, 1969. $15–$35*

Snoopy Musical Ge-tar. Picture on guitar depicts Snoopy sitting on a tree branch with a baseball in his mouth. Charlie Brown and Lucy, wearing baseball hats, are walking toward Snoopy. Crank the handle to play. The box front pictures the guitar. Plastic. Mattel, #4715, 1969. $15–$40*

Snoopy Musical Guitar. Turn the handle, listen to the music, watch Snoopy move his arms and Woodstock go up and down. The front of the guitar pictures a raised Snoopy and Woodstock. At the neck of the instrument are miniature figures of Snoopy, Charlie Brown, Woodstock, and Lucy. Window boxed. Plastic. Aviva, #444, 1980.

$20–$30*

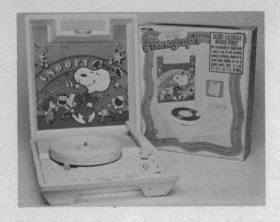

Snoopy phonograph (solid state). When the top is opened, a picture of Snoopy in a disco outfit, Peppermint Patty, Lucy, Charlie Brown, Linus, and Woodstock discoing are seen. The box cover has the same picture. Vanity Fair (a subsidiary of Walter Kidde & Company, Inc.), #66, 1979. $50–$60*

LEISURE

Big Quart-O-Snoopy Bubbles. Bubble wand and solution. Lucy, Charlie Brown, Snoopy, and Woodstock decorate the plastic wand. Second panel of bottle has dancing Snoopy thinking, "This Is My Big Bubble Dance." Chemtoy, late 1970s. $15–$20

Charlie Brown Deluxe Gift Pak. A cylindrical-shaped container with seven stereo reels and a stereo viewmaster. Box depicts Lucy, Woodstock, Charlie Brown, Sally, and Snoopy in his dancing pose. A little girl is holding the viewmaster. GAF/Viewmaster, #2380, late 1970s. $35–$45*

Kaleidorama. Caption: "Snoopy Disco." Scene depicted: Snoopy in disco suit all over the Kaleidorama doing different dance steps. He is joined by Woodstock. Put your eye to the opening at top and, by turning the bottom, you create designs using Snoopy, Woodstock, and brillant colors. Determined, #4961, 1979. $10–$20

Snoopy Movie Viewer. Simply insert the continuous color cartridge and crank forward or backward to see the animated Snoopy movies. Box depicts a child viewing a cassette in the green viewer with Snoopy on it as a movie director. Snoopy also appears on the box as a movie director. Kenner, #35900, 1975. $25–$40*

Snoopy's Bubble Blowing Bubble Tub. Box front: Snoopy submerged in a tub of bubbles captioned "Snoopy." The yellow extension pipe behind him resembles a shower nozzle. The tub is placed on a cardboard backdrop that can be hung on a wall. Pour some of the enclosed bubble liquid into the tub. When the red crank on the tub is turned and you blow into the end of the shower nozzle, bubbles are released. Chemtoy, late 1970s. $20–$35*

Snoopy's Fantastic Automatic Bubble Pipe. Plastic-wrapped package contains a bottle of bubble liquid and a red and white bubble pipe with a full-figure of Snoopy on top. Fill with liquid and, when you blow into the pipe, Snoopy rises and bubbles pour out. Chemtoy, #126, late 1970s. $12–$25*

MOTORIZED

Toy series. #500. Plastic. Aviva, 1978.

Charlie Brown, standing and wearing a red baseball hat, yellow shirt with a black zigzag design, black pants and shoes. 4¼".

$15–$25*

Snoopy as the Flying Ace wearing a green helmet, red scarf, and yellow goggles. 3¾". $10–$18*

Woodstock is sitting in a brown nest. 3". $10–$18*

Toy series. #966. Plastic. Aviva, 1977.

Lucy, rubber, is driving her gold-colored Doctor's Booth. Plastic. The front is captioned "Psychiatric Help 5¢. . . . The Doctor is IN." The sides are captioned "Lucy." $20–$30*

Snoopy, made of rubber, is in his Flying Ace outfit and driving his red and white doghouse. $10–$20*

Snoopy, made of rubber, is driving his red Desk-Mobile.

$15–$25*

Toy series. #500. Aviva, 1977.

Schroeder, rubber, drives his white Piano-Mobile. Side of piano is captioned "Schroeder." $25–$35*

Charlie Brown drives his brown baseball mound buggy. Side of mound captioned "Charlie Brown." $20–$30*

Linus drives his blue Blanket-Mobile. Side of Blanket-Mobile captioned "Linus." $25–$35*

Tug boat. Aviva/Hasbro, #575, 1978.

Snoopy and Woodstock, wearing captains' hats, are joined by Charlie Brown in a red and white tug boat. $20–$30*

Show boat. Snoopy and Woodstock are wearing captains' hats. Lucy joins them on the blue and white show boat with two big red wheels. $20–$30*

PLAY SETS

Batter Up, Snoopy. This is referred to as a standup play set. Front: Snoopy is wearing a baseball cap and carrying a bat and ball. Woodstock is walking with him. Colorforms, #304, 1979. $20–$25*

Camp Kamp. A half open log camp building with a red roof and yellow floor serves as a focal point for the members of the gang and their various camp activities. The characters are removable and interchangeable. This picture shows Snoopy, Schroeder, Lucy, and Linus canoeing while Charlie Brown and Peppermint Patty sit on a bench behind a picnic table. Stackable bunk beds and a campfire are also included. Rubber. Child Guidance, #1683, late 1970s.

$40–$55*

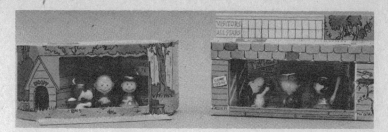

Charlie Brown's Backyard. Rubber figures of Snoopy, Lucy, and Charlie Brown in a brightly colored cardboard box. The backdrop is a backyard. The front of the box is cellophane and the back shows Peppermint Patty in a blow-up-type pool with Linus spraying water into it with a hose. Sally is in her sandbox. Child Guidance, #1733, late 1970s. $10–$15*

Charlie Brown's All Star Dugout. Rubber figures of Snoopy, Lucy, and Charlie Brown in a cardboard box with a locker room as the backdrop. Child Guidance, # 1636, late 1970s. $10–$15*

Lucy's Winter Carnival. Cover of box: Charlie Brown, Lucy, and Snoopy holding hands as they skate. Inside the box *Peanuts* characters appear in different winter activity poses to be placed on the cardboard snow and ice scene. Colorforms, #7400, 1973.

$12–$20*

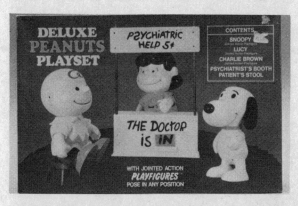

Peanuts Deluxe Play Set. Includes Lucy's psychiatrist booth, a stool, as well as Charlie Brown, Snoopy, and Lucy joined action figures. The sign in the front of her booth is captioned: "Psychiatric Help 5¢ . . . The Doctor Is In." The box cover shows the toy all set up. Plastic. Determined, #575, 1975. $75–$95*

Pop-Up. Three-dimensional, cardboard Happy Birthday, Snoopy. Box cover: a smiling Snoopy is the recipient of gifts, including a three-layer cake with Woodstock dancing on the top. Lucy, Linus, and Charlie Brown all share in the celebration. The set includes pressout figures of the *Peanuts* characters, place settings, party hats, and a happy birthday banner. Colorforms, #4107, 1974. $20–$35*

Peanuts Show Time Finger Puppets. Snoopy, Charlie Brown, Peppermint Patty, Linus, Lucy, and Woodstock are each a finger puppet made of rubber. The inside of the box is designed as a stage. Ideal, #5379-3, 1977. $10–$20*

Peanuts Stackables. These four hard rubber figures of Snoopy, Peppermint Patty, Lucy, and Charlie Brown are placed on top of each other. Woodstock is placed alongside of these fancy acrobats. Determined, #8642, 1979 (see photo on p. 288, bottom center). $15–$25*

Snoopy and His Doghouse. Snoopy is lying on his house and Woodstock is sitting on rim of Snoopy's supper dish. Snoopy is jointed and can be placed in many positions. Plastic. Determined, #476, 1975. $25–$40*

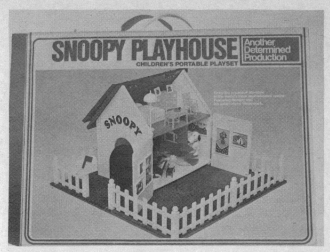

Snoopy Playhouse. A plastic replica of Snoopy's house. Miniature furniture includes a baby grand piano, desk with typewriter, chairs, light, paintings, etc., and of course the resident, a plastic-jointed Snoopy and his friend Woodstock. House is surrounded by a white fence. Boxed as a knock-down set. Determined, #120, 1977.

$80–$100*

Snoopy Playland. Snoopy is in a bus that moves along tracks and sets off different activities when he moves. Also included: Lucy, Linus, Schroeder, Charlie Brown, Peppermint Patty, and Woodstock. Box cover shows the playland all set up. Plastic. Aviva, #888, 1978.

$65–$75*

Snoopy Soaper. Push the button and Snoopy "clean hands inspector" dispenses a measured amount of soap (one 5-oz. packet included) to wash hands. The dispenser is gold colored with red trim. From the waist up, Snoopy is seen on top of the soaper. Caption: "Snoopy . . . Clean Hands Inspector." Plastic. Kenner, #30700, 1975. $20–$30*

Snoopy Stackables. These three hard rubber figures of Snoopy in different positions are to be placed one on top of the other. Determined, #8641, 1979 (see photo above, left). $10–$15*

Snoopy Tea Set. The tray features Lucy, Linus, Charlie Brown, Snoopy, Sally, Frieda, Pigpen, and Schroeder. The dinner plate has a picture of Linus with his blanket. Also included are two cups and saucers. These do not have any of the characters on them. Between the cups is a picture of Snoopy as the Flying Ace holding a cup of cocoa. The box is plastic wrapped and window boxed. Metal. J. Chein & Co., #276, 1970. $95–$120*

Snoopy's Beagle Scouts. A three-dimensional standup playset. Cover: scouts Lucy and Charlie Brown stack up logs for a fire as scoutmaster Snoopy leads Woodstock, who is holding a banner captioned "Troop 7." Colorforms, #4108, 1975. $20–$30*

Snoopy's Dog House. Wind up Snoopy and he walks on top of the roof to raise the flag and even rides the ice cream car. Wind up Woodstock and he hops, pretending to sip from the bird bath. Romper Room/Hasbro, #815, 1978. $25–$35*

Snoopy's Soft House. When the soft cloth house is closed it can be carried as a handbag. When opened, it includes: Snoopy, Woodstock, a sleeping bag, soft stuffed chair, nightshirt, nightcap, vest, scarf. The box cover depicts a little girl with the soft house set up and she is playing with it. Knickerbocker, #0573, 1980.

$15–$25*

Snoopy's Swim & Sail Club. The characters included are: Charlie Brown, Linus, Snoopy, Woodstock, and Lucy. To complete the set, plastic lifeguard station, boats, water skis, surfboard, and surf shop are also included. Child Guidance, #1710, late 1970s. $50–$60*

Tub Time Snoopy. The rubber doll in this toy comes with a red bathrobe and scrub brush. He is tubable, washable, and jointed. Window boxed. Knickerbocker, #0539, early 1980s. $15–$25*

Yankee Doodle Snoopy. The box cover depicts Snoopy in a tricornered hat and holding a flag. Woodstock is wearing an Uncle Sam hat. Colorforms, #756, 1975. $4–$15*

Hold That Line, Charlie Brown! The box cover features Charlie Brown running with a football. Lucy is in the background as a cheerleader. Colorforms, #753, 1974. $7–$15*

PRESCHOOL

Copter Pull, Snoopy. This is a sound and action pull toy featuring Snoopy and Woodstock. Snoopy's soft ears spin around as he's pulled along. Has "boing-boing" sound. Plastic. Romper Room, #822, 1980. $4–$20*

Peanuts Play Set. Preschool colorforms with larger pieces. Box cover: Snoopy and Woodstock standing on Snoopy's house. Charlie Brown and Lucy stand in front. Rainbow is behind them. Colorforms, #8110, 1980. $10–$20*

Push 'N' Fly, Snoopy. Pushed along the floor, Snoopy, on the handle as the Flying Ace, flies up and down. Woodstock watches the action through binoculars. Decals of Woodstock appear on three sides of the orange base. Plastic. Romper Room/Hasbro, #824, 1980.
                                                        $20–$30

Snoopy the Chef. This toy includes a 5″-jointed vinyl Snoopy, plastic Woodstock, chef's hat and apron, stool and sink unit, spoon, frying pan, pot with lid, coffee pot, and a cake. Window boxed. Knickerbocker, #9740-0542, 5″, 1979. $35–$50*

Snoopy the Astronaut. This toy includes a 5″-vinyl jointed Snoopy, plastic Woodstock, space suit, helmet, moon shoes, camera, life support system, American flag, moon rover vehicle. Knickerbocker, #9740-0540, 5″, 1979. $25–$35*

Snoopy the Sport. This toy includes a 5″-jointed vinyl Snoopy, plastic Woodstock, two-piece warm-up suit, two-piece tennis outfit, sneakers, socks, sun visor, tennis tote, two tennis rackets, soccer ball, and terry towel. Knickerbocker, #9740-6541, 5″, 1979.

$25–$35*

Snoopy Jack-in-the-Box. This is the only jack-in-the-box with double popping action. Turn crank and play "Pop Goes the Beagle." Woodstock pops up from his nest and Snoopy pops through the front door. Romper Room/Hasbro, #818, 1980. $15–$25*

PUPPETS

Peanuts Magic Catch Puppets. Synergistics, 1978 (see the following descriptions for the above photo, left to right).

Lucy. Wears a blue dress. The material of her outfit and the velcro ball enable her to be a game as well as a puppet. #SP40.

$12–$20*

Woodstock. Wears a green and orange shirt captioned "Woodstock ½." The material of Woodstock's outfit and the velcro ball enable him to be a game as well as a puppet. #SP30. $12–$20*

Snoopy. Wears a green and yellow shirt captioned "Snoopy 1." The material of Snoopy's outfit and the velcro ball enable him to be a game as well as a puppet. #SP20. $12–$20*

Charlie Brown. Chuck is wearing an orange, white, and blue baseball shirt captioned "Charlie Brown #47." The material of his outfit and the velcro ball enable him to be a game as well as a puppet. #SP10. $12–$20*

Peanuts Pelham Puppets. Made in England. Pelham/Tiderider, 1979.

Charlie Brown. Wears black pants, orange shoes, and orange shirt, all of which are painted on. His hat is orange felt, but it cannot come off easily. #SS19, 8″. $40–$50*

Snoopy. Wears a red collar. Black felt ears. #SS18, 8″. $25–$35*

Woodstock, who has felt wings. #SS20, 7″. $25–$35

A big Snoopy. He is wearing a red cloth shirt and blue jeans. He has a baseball glove on his left hand and a baseball is suspended on a string to reach his glove. #DP10, 27″. $350–$400

Peanuts Puppets Display. Most probably bought by stores that were selling the puppets. This was a good attention getter and displayed the puppets to their full advantage. The sign behind the puppets reads "Pelham Puppets, Loved by Children All Over the World—Marlborough—Wilshire, England." The puppets displayed are Snoopy, Woodstock, and Charlie Brown. Plug it in and watch the puppets dance. Pelham/Tiderider, 1979. $275–$350

SPORTS

My Friend Snoopy. This plastic bowling toy comes with a 14″ Snoopy, ten bowling pins, two balls, and a bowling mat. You can pull back Snoopy's hand and he will throw you the ball. You can pull back his arm and he'll knock down the pins. He's very athletic! You can also move his ears and turn his head. Romper Room/Hasbro, #825, 1979. $10–$25*

Official Peanuts Baseball. Snoopy, Charlie Brown, Linus, and Schroeder appear on the baseball. Box: Front: Schroeder, Charlie Brown, Snoopy with his supper dish in his mouth on the baseball mound. Back: Charlie Brown, Linus, and Lucy. Side: Schroeder and Snoopy. Opposite side: Snoopy, Charlie Brown, and Linus. In all the pictures the gang is in baseball gear. Wilson Sporting Goods, 1969. $60–$80*

Snoopy All Star Catch Mitt. Each finger on the mitt has a picture of a *Peanuts* character on it. When the enclosed ball (with velcro strips) is thrown, it sticks to the special fabric of the mitt. Synergistics, series "SM," 1977. $20–$30*

Snoopy Slugger. Complete set consists of an oversized "Official *Peanuts* Baseball," yellow bat with a picture of Snoopy, and orange and white cap, also featuring Snoopy. Plastic with cloth cap. Playskool, #411, 1979. $20–$30*

TRANSPORTATION

Die-cast vehicles (part 1). Aviva, #700, 4¾", 1977 (originally).

Snoopy's airplane. Snoopy as the Flying Ace pilots his yellow biplane with red wings, appropriately named "Snoopy." A decal of Woodstock is on the tail. $10–$25*

Snoopy's family car. Charlie Brown is the driver of this orange convertible with green and gray plastic accents. Snoopy and Lucy are in the back seat and Woodstock is behind them. $35–$45*

Snoopy's sports car. Snoopy drives a yellow convertible with red and green accents while Woodstock sits on the back. $20–$30*

Die-cast vehicles (part 2). Aviva, #700, 4¾", 1977 (originally).

Snoopy's racer. Snoopy, in a red helmet, is the driver of a blue "Formula 1" race car. The name "Snoopy" appears on both sides and the back. $20–$40

Snoopy's locomotive. Snoopy leans out of the cab of a blue locomotive with red trim. $20–$35*

Snoopy's fire engine. Snoopy drives a red hook and ladder fire truck. $20–$35*

Die-cast vehicles ("Snoopy Handfuls Set"). Hasbro/Aviva, #2036, 2½", 1980. $30–$45* set

Woodstock is driving a white ice cream truck with blue and red trim. Decals on each side captioned "Snoopy" and picture an ice cream cone.

Snoopy is driving a green truck which carries his red and white house in the back. Decals on both sides of the house captioned "Snoopy."

Snoopy is driving a blue U.S. mail truck. Both sides show Snoopy's paw print. Caption: "Snoopy U.S. Mail."

Die-cast vehicles ("Emergency Set"). Hasbro/Aviva, #2036, 2½", 1980. $30–$45* set

Snoopy is driving his red fire truck with yellow plastic accents.

Snoopy is driving his purple snorkel with yellow plastic accents.

Snoopy is driving his silver wrecker with red and blue accents and a red plastic lift in the back.

Freewheeling action ("Snoopy Freewheeling Action Set"). Aviva/ Hasbro, #2038, 1980. $40–$50* set

Lucy in her yellow racer with silver "chrome" accents. On the front hood is a red decal captioned "15."

Woodstock in his red and white racer with a large silver tailpipe.

Snoopy in his red racer with silver "chrome" accents. On the front hood is a decal captioned "4."

Woodstock in his green racer with silver "chrome" accents. On the front hood is a decal captioned "1."

Freewheeling. (Freewheeling Snoopy and Friend on Skateboard). Plastic. Aviva, #757, 4" l., 1977.

Snoopy as the Flying Ace, Woodstock in his nest on a red skateboard. $6–$9*

Charlie Brown, Woodstock in his nest on a red skateboard.
$6–$9*

Snoopy, as a skater, is wearing blue shorts. Woodstock is in his nest. Together, they are on a blue skateboard. $6–$9*

Snoopy as Joe Cool is wearing a yellow shirt. Woodstock is in his nest. They are both on a yellow skateboard. $6–$9*

Snoopy, Charlie Brown, and Woodstock are on a blue skateboard. $6–$9*

Snoopy as the Flying Ace and Charlie Brown are on a yellow skateboard. $6–$9*

Mini die-cast vehicles (part 1). Aviva, #2030, approximately 2½″, 1977 (originally).

Lucy drives an orange jeep that resembles her psychiatrist booth. The front is captioned "Psychiatric Help 5¢. . . . The Doctor is IN." $4–$12*

Snoopy is driving a green truck with his doghouse in the back. (Also in assortment #2033.) $4–$12*

Woodstock is driving a white ice cream truck with decals of ice cream on each side. (Also in Handfuls set #2036.) $4–$12*

Mini die-cast vehicles (part 2). Aviva, #2030, approximately 2½″ l., 1977 (originally).

Snoopy is driving his surf buggy with his surfboard on top, captioned "Snoopy." $4–$12*

Snoopy is driving his tow truck. $4–$12*

Woodstock is driving his red forklift with the front loader in yellow. $4–$12*

Mini die-cast vehicles (part 3). Aviva, #2030, approximately 2½″ l., 1977 (originally).

Woodstock drives a blue and yellow covered wagon with red wheels. $4–$12*

Snoopy driving a red racer. $4–$12*

Charlie Brown is driving a red and white racer. $4–$12*

Snoopy is driving a blue racer. $4–$12*

Charlie Brown is driving a blue pick-up truck. In the back he is carrying his bat and glove. $4–$12*

Snoopy is driving a red fire engine with yellow plastic trim and yellow plastic ladders on each side. (Also in assortment #2033.) $4–$12*

Mini die-cast vehicles (part 1). Aviva, #2033, approximately 2½″, 1977 (originally).

Snoopy driving a yellow ski buggy. The carrier on top holds the skis. Captioned "Snoopy." The sticker on the hood shows a picture of a snowman and reads "Ski." $4–$12*

Snoopy is driving his blue fun van with red trim. The psychedelic sticker on each side is captioned "Fun Van." A sticker on the top reads "Snoopy." $4–$12*

Snoopy driving a red racer with #61 on the hood. The rear is captioned "Snoopy." $4–$12*

Mini die-cast vehicles (part 2). Aviva, #2033, approximately 2½″, 1977 (originally).

Snoopy is driving a green truck carrying his red and white doghouse in the back. $4–$12*

Snoopy is driving a red and yellow Cat Catcher truck. The decal wrapped around the back shows a butterfly net and reads "Snoopy." $4–$12*

Snoopy is driving his red and yellow snorkel. Snoopy is sitting in a lift that can be raised and lowered. $4–$12*

Mini die-cast vehicles (part 3). Aviva, #2033, approximately 2½″, 1977 (originally).

Woodstock is driving his land rover. $4–$12*

Charlie Brown drives a red locomotive with a blue and yellow trim. $4–$12*

Lucy drives her yellow racer with #15 on the front. $4–$12*

Woodstock drives a green racer. $4–$12*

Snoopy drives his green truck. $4–$12*

Snoopy is driving a red fire engine with plastic yellow trim and yellow ladders on each side. (Also in assortment #2030.)

$4–$12*

Oversized characters in large die-cast vehicles. Aviva/Hasbro, 4³/₄", mid 1980s.

Snoopy, wearing a red helmet, drives a red hook and ladder fire truck. Woodstock sits in the rear. #72039/1. $8–$12*

Snoopy, in red helmet, is the driver of a blue "Formula 1" race car. The name "Snoopy" appears on both sides and the back. #72039/3. $8–$12*

Snoopy drives a yellow convertible with red and green accents while Woodstock sits on the back. #72039/2. $8–$12*

Snoopy as the Flying Ace pilots his yellow biplane with red wings, appropriately named "Snoopy." A decal of Woodstock is on the tail of the plane. $8–$12*

An asterisk (*) next to a price indicates that the item comes with its original box in excellent condition. If no asterisk is shown, there is no box or the box adds little significant value. Shipping boxes (no graphics) are of no value.

A copyright date indicates the year the character first appeared in a particular incarnation, *not* the year the product first came out.

Oversized characters in mini die-cast vehicles. Hasbro PreSchool, 2½", early 1980s.

Snoopy, wearing a black tuxedo and top hat, drives a yellow open car. #72044-2. $4–$8*

Snoopy as the Flying Ace drives a red racer. #72044-6. $4–$8*

Snoopy in a red hat drives a truck called "Cat Catcher." #72044-5. $4–$8*

Snoopy, wearing a red fire helmet, drives a red fire truck. #72044-3. $4–$8*

Charlie Brown, red cap turned sideways, drives a yellow open car. #72044-1. $4–$8*

Woodstock drives a circus wagon. #72077-4. $4–$8*

Oversized characters in mini die-cast vehicles. Packaged as a set and captioned "Snoopy Happy Die-cast." Packed in a window box. Top flap shows Lucy, Charlie Brown, and Snoopy playing with the die-casts. Hasbro, 2½", early 1980s. $30–$38* set

Snoopy, wearing a red fire helmet, drives a red fire truck. #72044-3.

Snoopy, wearing a black tuxedo and top hat, drives a yellow open car. #72044-2.

Snoopy as the Flying Ace drives a red racer. #72044-6.

Snoopy Biplane (mini die-cast). Snoopy appears as the Flying Ace in his mini die-cast biplane captioned "Snoopy." Came with either yellow or red wings. Sits on a heavy paper platform decorated with Snoopy as the Flying Ace. Covered with a removable plastic cover. Aviva, #2024, 1¾", 1977. $15-$20*

Snoopy Family Car (mini die-cast toy). Snoopy, with Charlie Brown sitting next to him, drives a convertible car. Lucy and Woodstock sit in the back. The car sits on a lightweight cardboard base with a removable plastic covering. Aviva, #2028, 2¼", 1977. $15-$25*

MIB (Mint In Box): Item in unopened box, box in excellent condition.

Mint Condition: Superior quality, box missing.

Good Condition: All parts are included. Item and/or box shows limited wear and tear.

Poor Condition: Major wear and tear. Parts may be missing.

Snoopy Push 'N' Pull Toys. There's Snoopy's rescue truck, ice cream truck, helicopter, and car captioned "#2." The characters—Snoopy as Flying Ace, Snoopy with fireman's hat, Charlie Brown with red baseball hat, Woodstock, and two extra characters, Snoopy and Lucy—are interchangeable in the vehicles. Originally produced in 1977 with four vehicles and four characters. Plastic. Window box. Aviva, #70850, 1982. $25–$40*

Snoopy Skate 'N' Surf (mini die-cast). Each character is on a metal skateboard. Aviva, #2044, 1977. $35–$55* set

Snoopy as the Flying Ace sits on a blue skateboard.

Charlie Brown, wearing a red baseball cap, stands on a red skateboard.

Woodstock sits in his nest on a red skateboard.

Snoopy the Surfer wears blue shorts with a red and yellow trim as he stands on a green skateboard.

Wagons, metal (part I). Aviva, #2055, 1¾", 1977.

Snoopy in a red wagon captioned "Snoopy." $12–$16*

Woodstock is in an orange wagon captioned "Woodstock." $12–$16*

Charlie Brown is in a blue wagon captioned "Charlie Brown" (see photo on previous page, bottom right). $12–$16*

Wagons, metal (part II). Aviva, #2055, 1¾", 1977. $12–$16*

Snoopy as Joe Cool is in a purple wagon captioned "Joe Cool."
                                                          $12–$16*

Snoopy and Woodstock are in a green wagon captioned "Snoopy and Woodstock." $12–$16*

Snoopy as the Flying Ace in a yellow wagon captioned "Flying Ace." $12–$16*

Wooden vehicles. Aviva, #100, 1977.

Snoopy's Fish Truck. Decals at window show Snoopy in a yellow rain slicker and hat. Decals on side say "Snoopy's Fish Truck" and another sign on the side says "Fish." #WT 003. $18–$25*

Snoopy's Bug. A decal of Snoopy's head wearing Flying Ace gear depicts him as the driver. A blue and red striped decal runs over the front, top, and back of the car. There are racing decals on both sides. Red plastic wheels. #WT 001. $18–$25*

Joe Cool's Car. There is a decal of Joe Cool on each side at the window. The decal in back says "Rah." Decals on the side say "Joe Cool." #WT 002. $18–$25*

WIND-UP

Action toys. Plastic. Aviva, 1977.

Snoopy the Drummer. Snoopy is wearing a parade hat and plays the drums after he is wound up with a big yellow plastic key. Woodstock is sitting on the drum. #833. $25–$40*

The Champ. Snoopy is wearing red boxing gloves and, when he is wound up with a big yellow key, he beats the punching bag upon which Woodstock is sitting. #836. $25–$40*

World's Greatest Cook. Snoopy as a chef is holding a frying pan in his hand. When he is wound up with a big plastic yellow key he flips the toy egg. #835. $4–$20*

Snoopy Express Mechanical Wind-Up Train Set. Plastic. Snoopy is the engineer in his locomotive, captioned "Snoopy Express," which is connected to the passenger car carrying Peppermint Patty, Charlie Brown, and Snoopy (paper decals). Woodstock is in his nest on top of the passenger car. Snoopy's doghouse, with Snoopy lying on top, is connected to the passenger car. Aviva, #70911, 1982. $15–$25*

Snoopy Express Mechanical Wind-Up Wood Train. Snoopy, as an engineer, is running the locomotive captioned "Snoopy's Express." The connected car seats Charlie Brown, Peppermint Patty, and Woodstock. Snoopy is in the last car in his dancing pose. Aviva, #911, 1977.   *$20–$80**

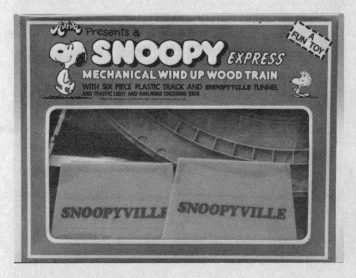

Snoopy Express Mechanical Wind-Up Wood Train. A train and track set. A complete set has the Snoopy three-piece wind-up train; two cars carrying Charlie Brown, Peppermint Patty, and Woodstock are coupled to the locomotive with Snoopy as the engineer. Also included is a six-piece track set, two signal signs, and a plastic Snoopyville tunnel. Aviva, #922, 1977.   *$65–$100**

Snoopy Skis. Arms and poles move in a skiing action as the toy is in motion. Aviva, #711, 1979.

Lucy is wearing a blue dress, lavender pants, and a ski hat. She is standing on green skis with Woodstock between the skis.

$18–$25*

Snoopy is wearing a red hat and yellow sweater and is on red skis with Woodstock standing between the skis. $18–$25*

Charlie Brown is wearing a yellow sweater with a black zigzag design, black pants, red hat and is on red skis with Woodstock between the skis. $18–$25*

Snoopy VS the Red Baron. A hard cardboard Snoopy, as the Flying Ace, is sitting on top of his plastic red house. Wind up the house by turning the metal key and it jumps up and down and around. Chein, #139, late 1960s. $30–$50*

Walkers, plastic. Wind up the small knob and Woodstock hops while the others walk. Aviva, 1975–1982.

Snoopy, 3″. $1–$3*

Joe Cool, 3″. $2–$6*

Toreador, 3″. $6–$10*

Woodstock, 2¾″. $1–$3*

Walkers, plastic. Aviva, 1975.

Woodstock with an Indian feather, 3½″. $3–$6*

Snoopy as a tennis player, 3″. $3–$5*

Snoopy as a football player, 3″. $3–$6*

Belle, 3″. $6–$10*

Snoopy as a sheriff, 3″. $3–$6*

Snoopy wearing a tux and top hat, 3½″. $3–$6*

Snoopy as the Flying Ace, 3″. $2–$5*

Walkers, plastic. Wind up the little knob and Woodstock hops and Snoopy walks. Aviva, 1975.

Snoopy as Joe Cool, 4¼″. $2–$5*

Woodstock with a red nightcap on, 3½″. $3–$6*

Snoopy wears a red stocking cap with a white pompom, 3½″.

                                                                $3–$6*

A Final Word from the Authors

The first effort must certainly be the most difficult.

The massive amount of research, the hours of typing, proofreading, and just plain shuffling papers involved far more of everything than we could possibly envision. But as the old saw goes, it was a labor of love.

We learned a lot while we were doing it. One of the things we learned was that we could not adequately cover the field in one volume. We hope in the near future to come out with a second volume which will include new items and new information to assist the collector.

If you have any comments about this edition or anything you would like to see in the next one, please write and tell us about it. If you have a favorite collectible that was not included and you would like us to consider it for publication, please send us a picture. Finally, if you have any questions on *Peanuts* collecting or memorabilia, we would be happy to answer them for you. All we ask is that you send one of us an S.A.S.E. (self-addressed stamped envelope). We cannot guarantee return of pictures but we do promise you will receive a reply.

Andrea Podley
P.O. Box 94
North Hollywood, CA 91603

Freddi Margolin
P.O. Box 5124 P
Bay Shore, NY 11706

Recommended Reading for Fun and Information

The following books go into considerable detail about the life and art of Charles M. Schulz.

Charlie Brown & Charlie Schulz, by Charles M. Schulz and Lee Mendelson, World Publishing Co., 1969.

Charlie Brown, Snoopy & Me, by Charles M. Schulz and R. Smith Killiper, Doubleday, New York, 1980.

Good Grief. The Story of Charles M. Schulz, by Rheta Grinsley Johnson, Pharos Books, New York, 1989.

Happy Birthday, Charlie Brown, by Charles M. Schulz and Lee Mendelson, Random House, New York, 1979.

Peanuts Jubilee, by Charles M. Schulz, Holt, Rinehart & Winston, New York, 1975.

You Don't Look 35, Charlie Brown, by Charles M. Schulz, Holt, Rinehart & Winston, New York, 1985.

Index

COLLECT COMICS!!

The *Official®* Overstreet Comic Book Price Guide
Companion, in its *third* edition, written by expert
ROBERT OVERSTREET, *tells us how!*

★ This portable, easy-to-carry treasure includes the *complete*
guide to BIG LITTLE BOOKS... lists today's prices of the *most*
collectible comic books... features a comic book convention
calendar... with cover art by artist John Buscema!

This is a treasure chest of all your favorite comics!

Fourth edition coming soon!

HOUSE OF COLLECTIBLES
201 East 50th Street
New York, New York 10022

Please send me *The Official®* Overstreet Comic Book Price
Guide Companion, 3rd Ed.... 0-876-37799-1 ... $4.95. I am
enclosing $_____ (add 50¢ per copy to cover
postage and handling). Send check or money order—no
cash or C.O.D.'s, please. Prices and numbers are subject to
change without notice.

Name _____

Address _____

City _____ State _____ Zip Code _____

Allow at least 4 weeks for delivery.